FLY IN THE SKY

A photo Experience
Robert Ornig

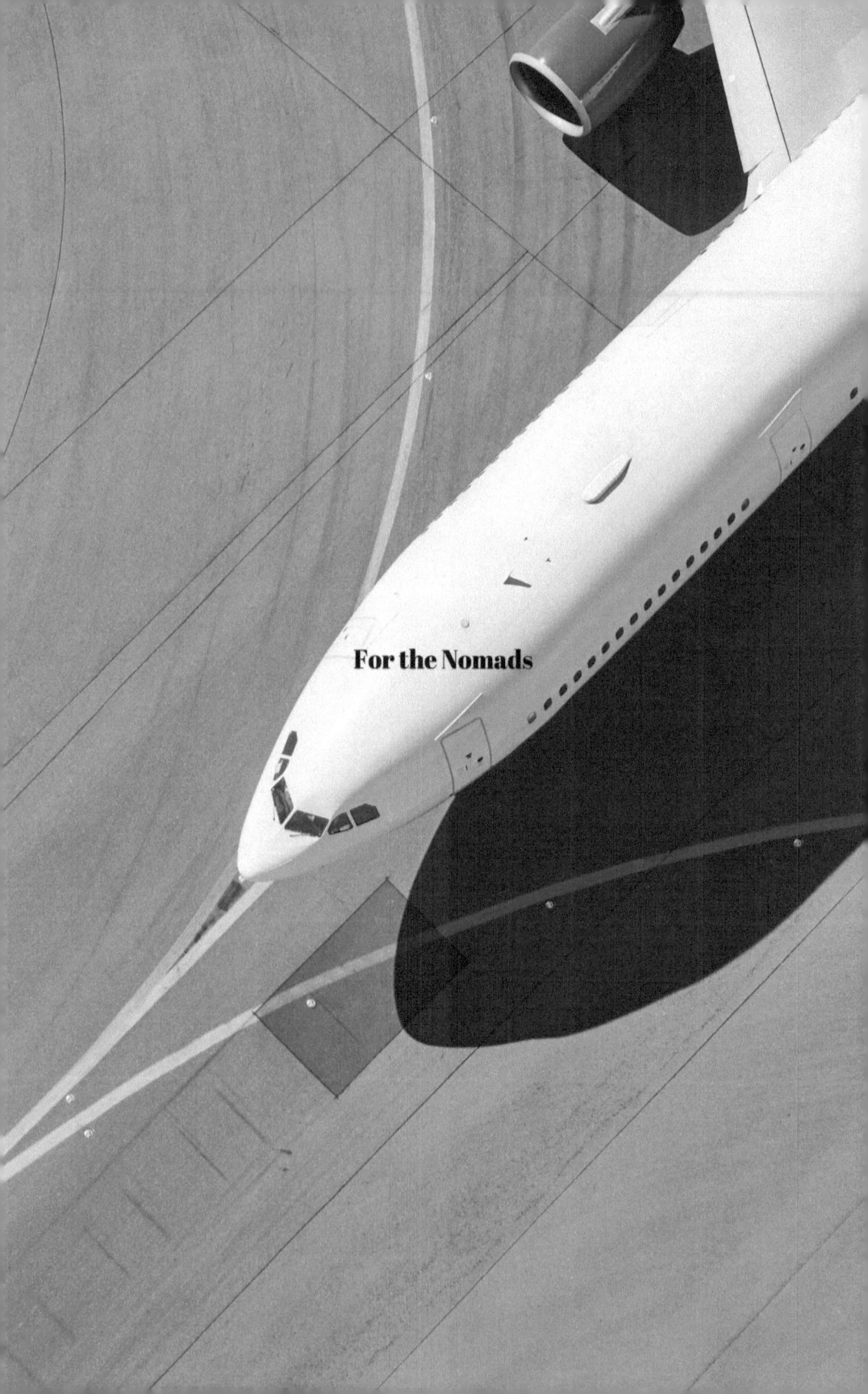

For the Nomads

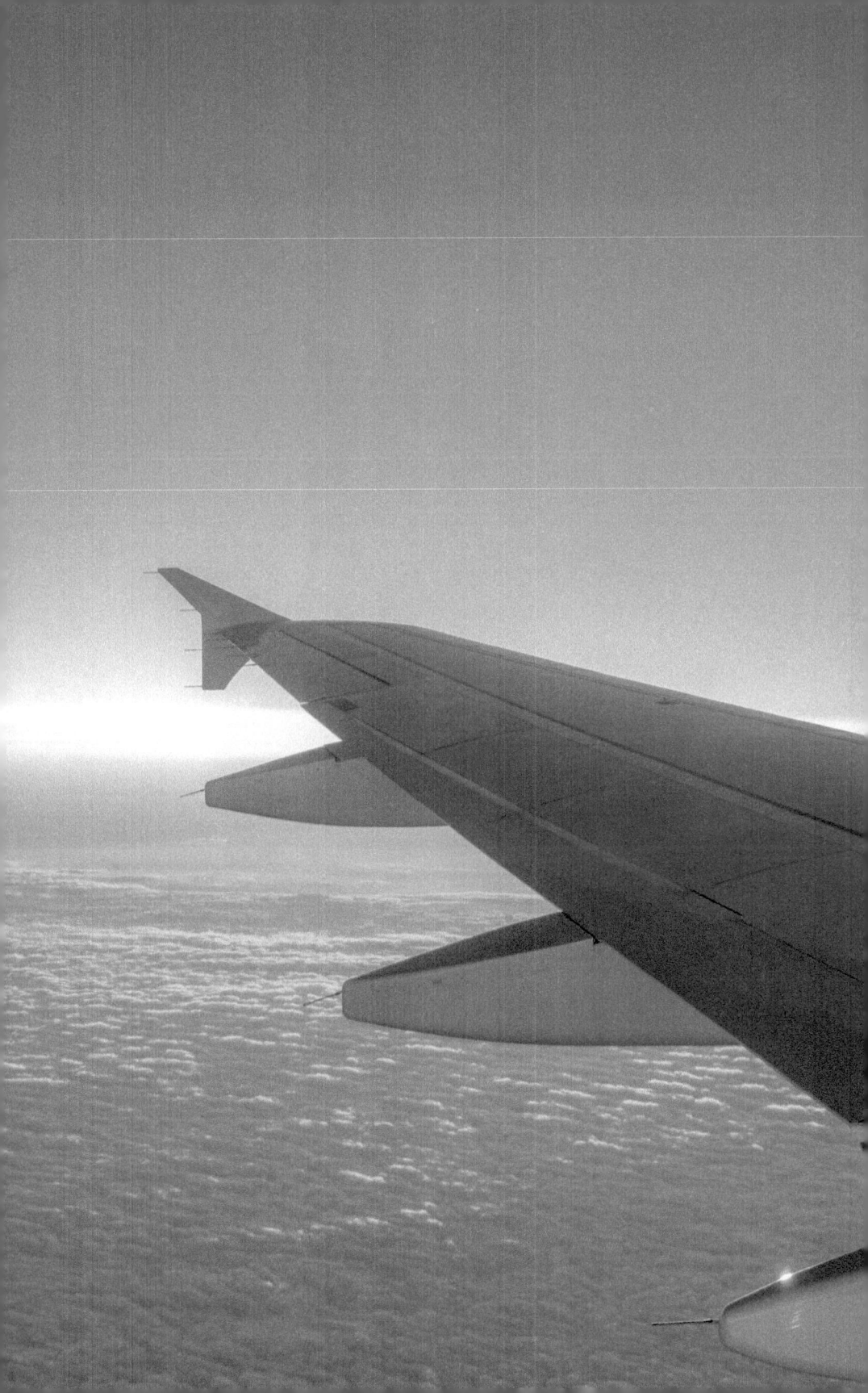

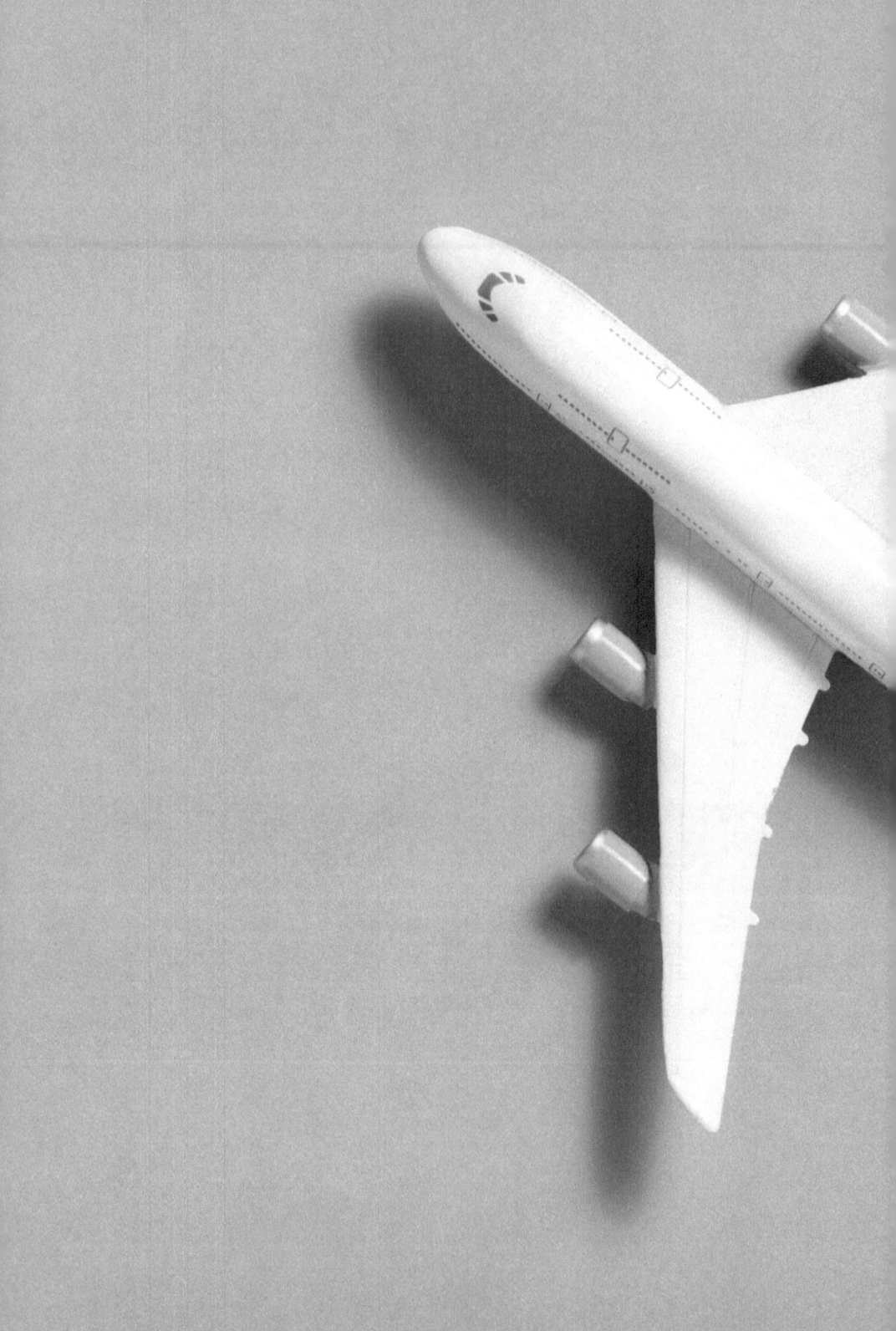

"The Guide says there is an art to flying", said Ford, "or rather a knack. The knack lies in learning how to throw yourself at the ground and miss."

Douglas Adams

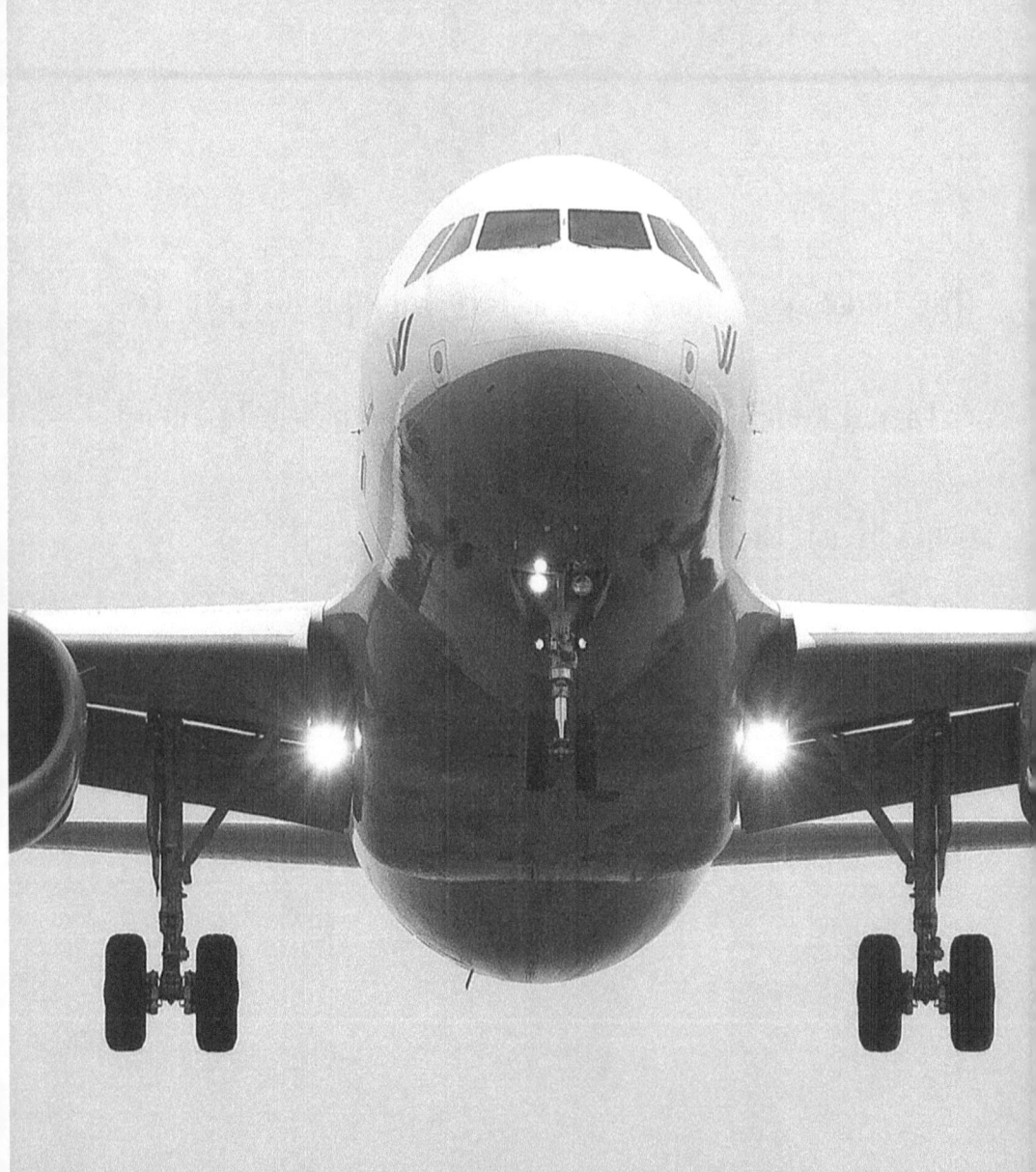

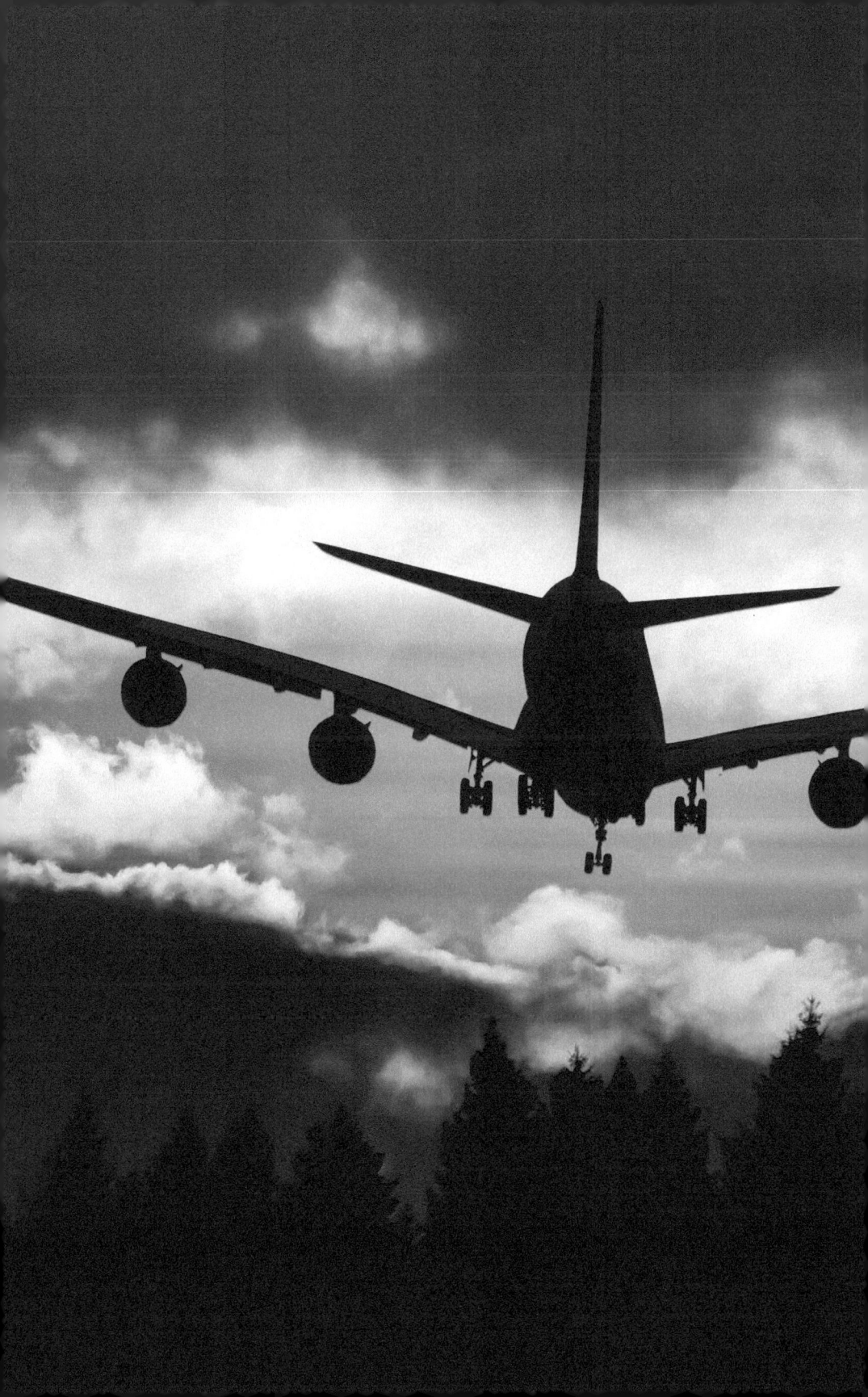

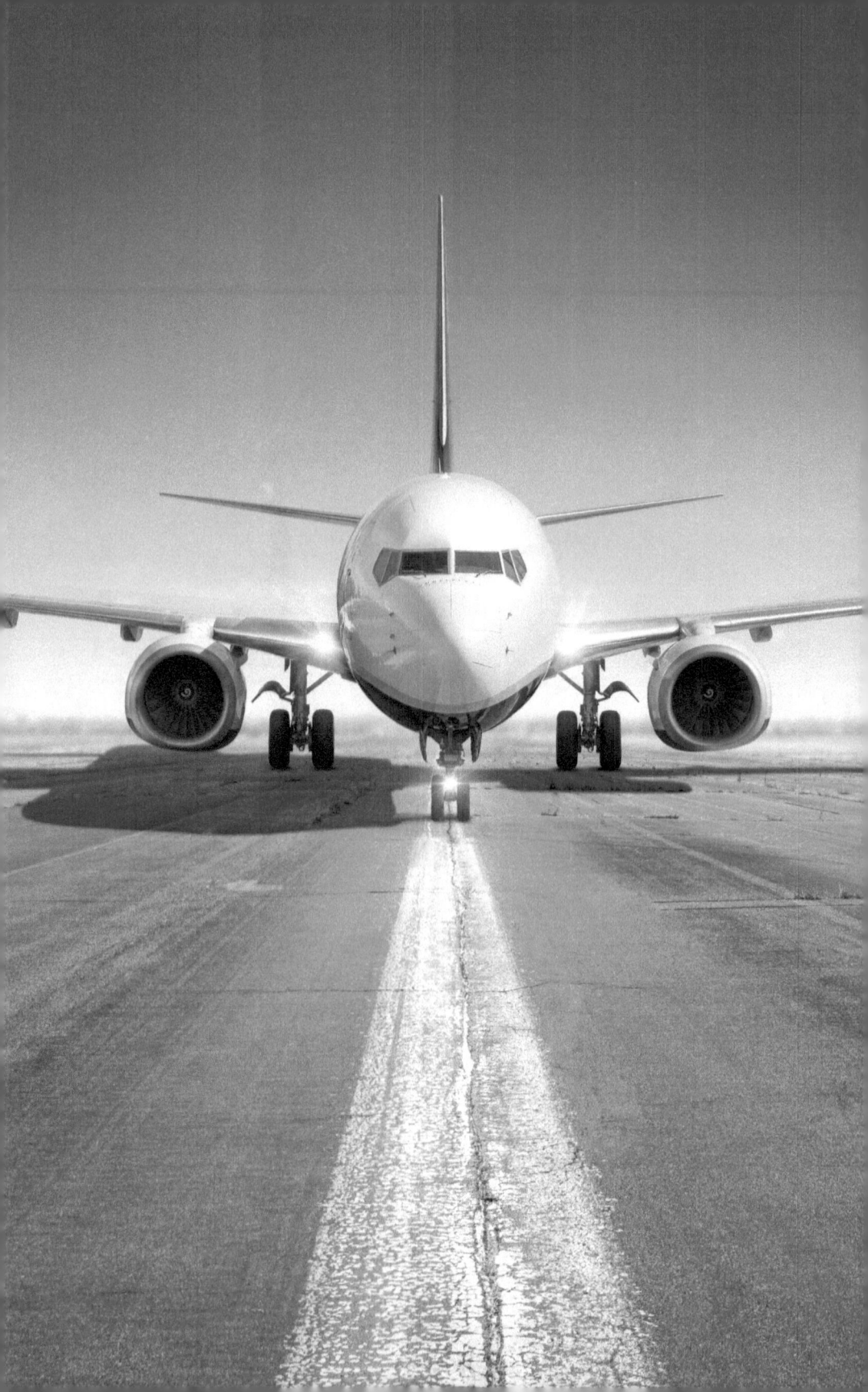

"Once you have tasted flight, you will forever walk the earth with your eyes turned skyward, for there you have been, and there you will always long to return."

Leonardo da Vinci

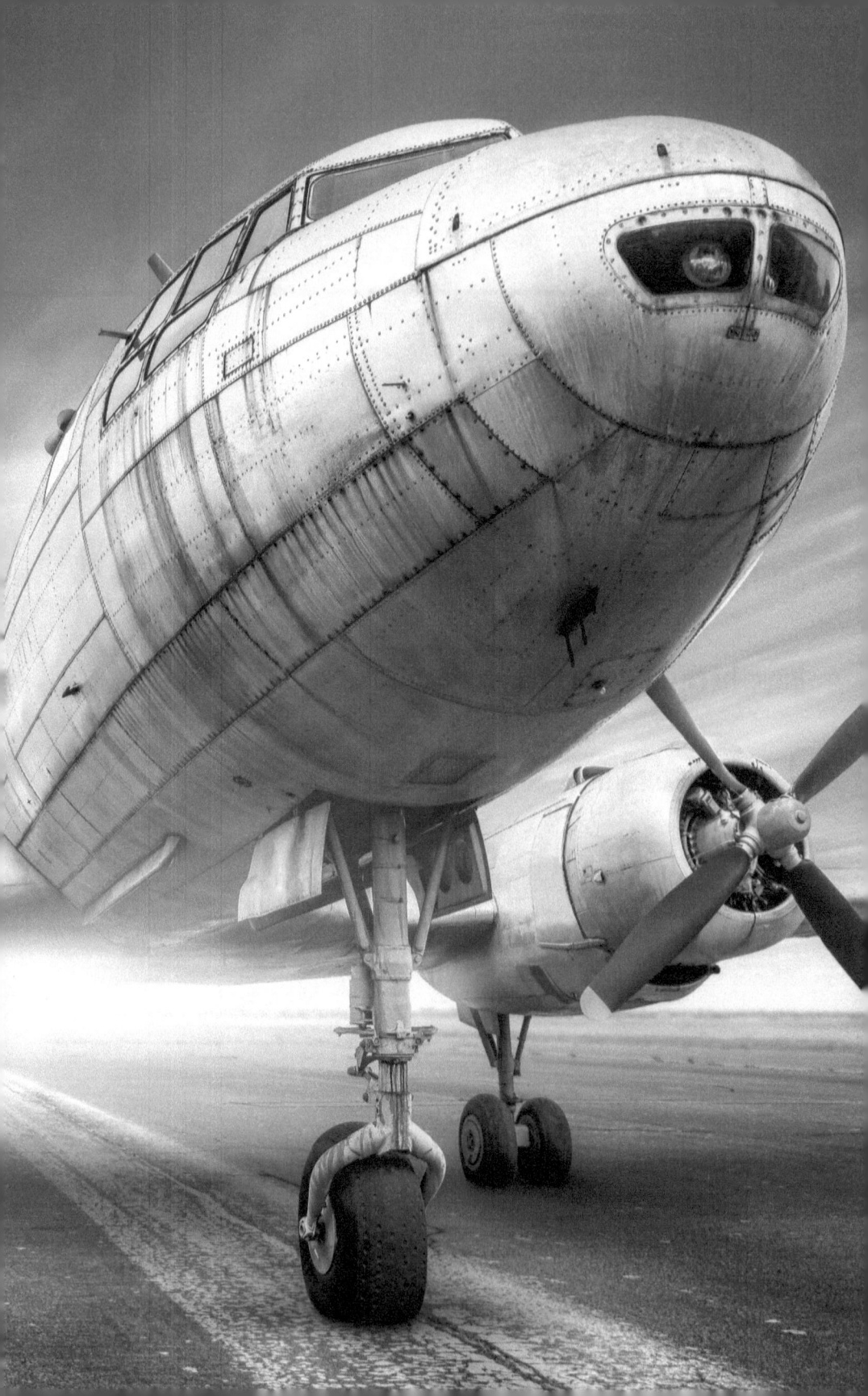

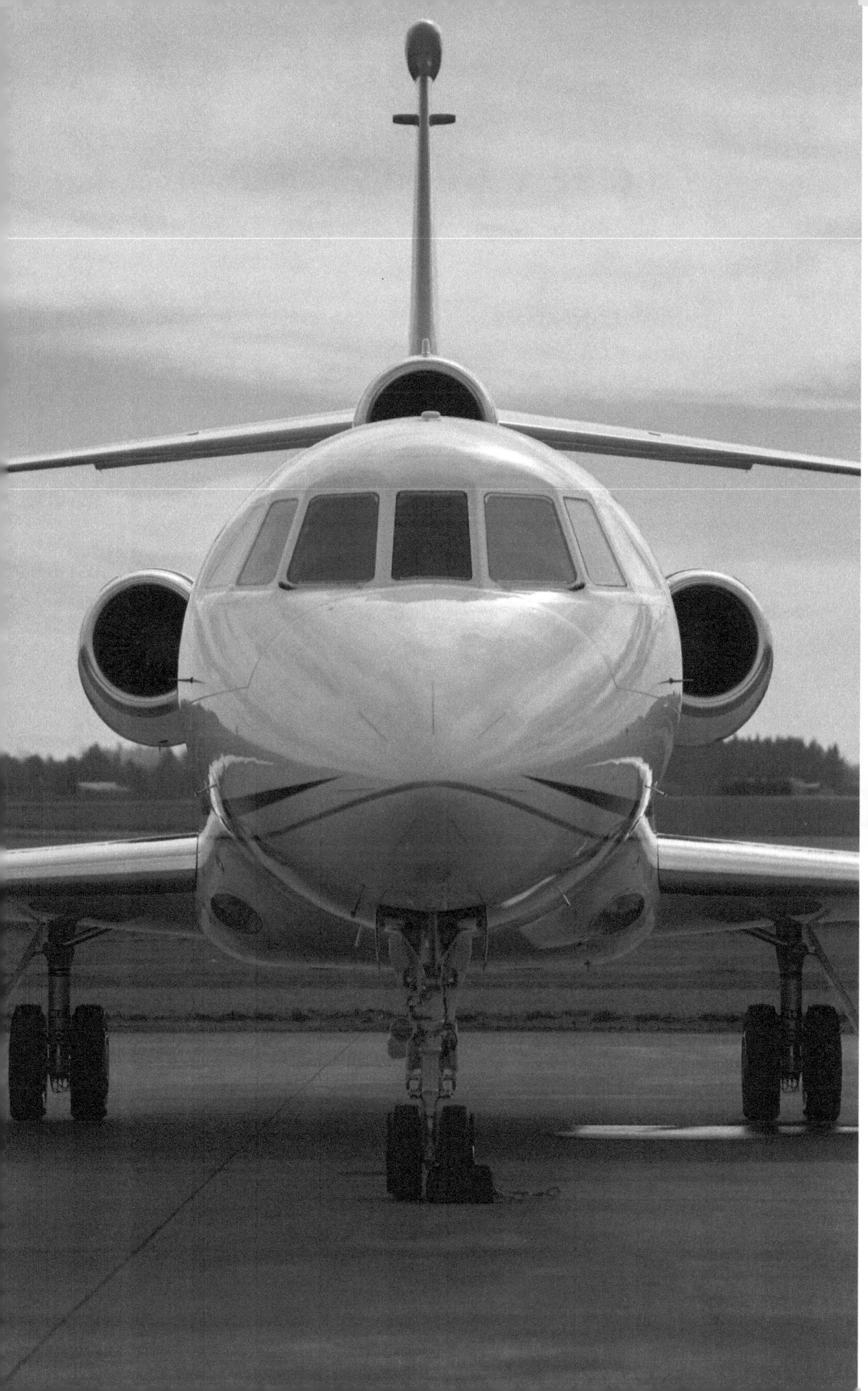

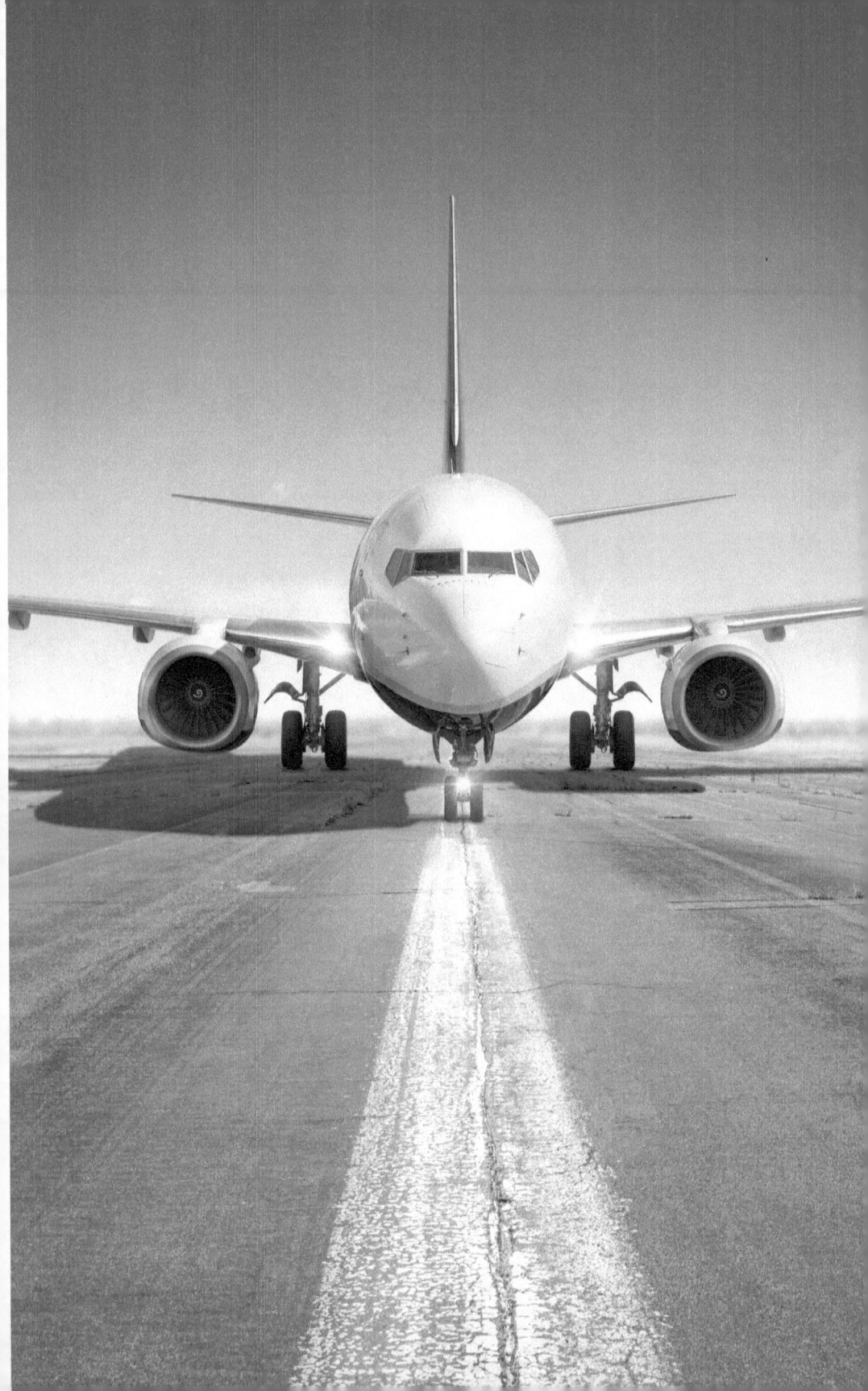

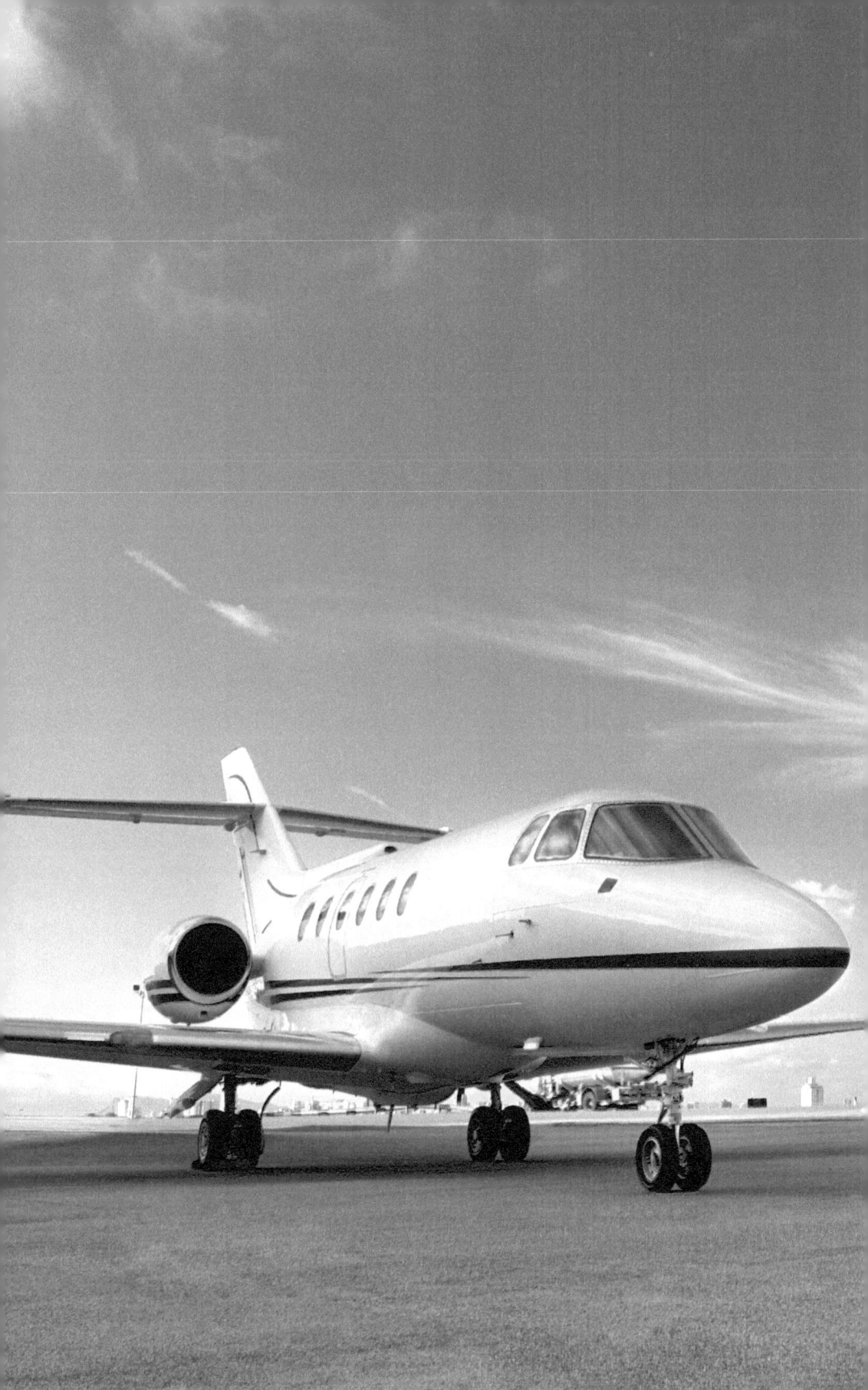

"The moment you doubt whether you can fly, you cease for ever to be able to do it."

J. M. Barrie, Peter Pan

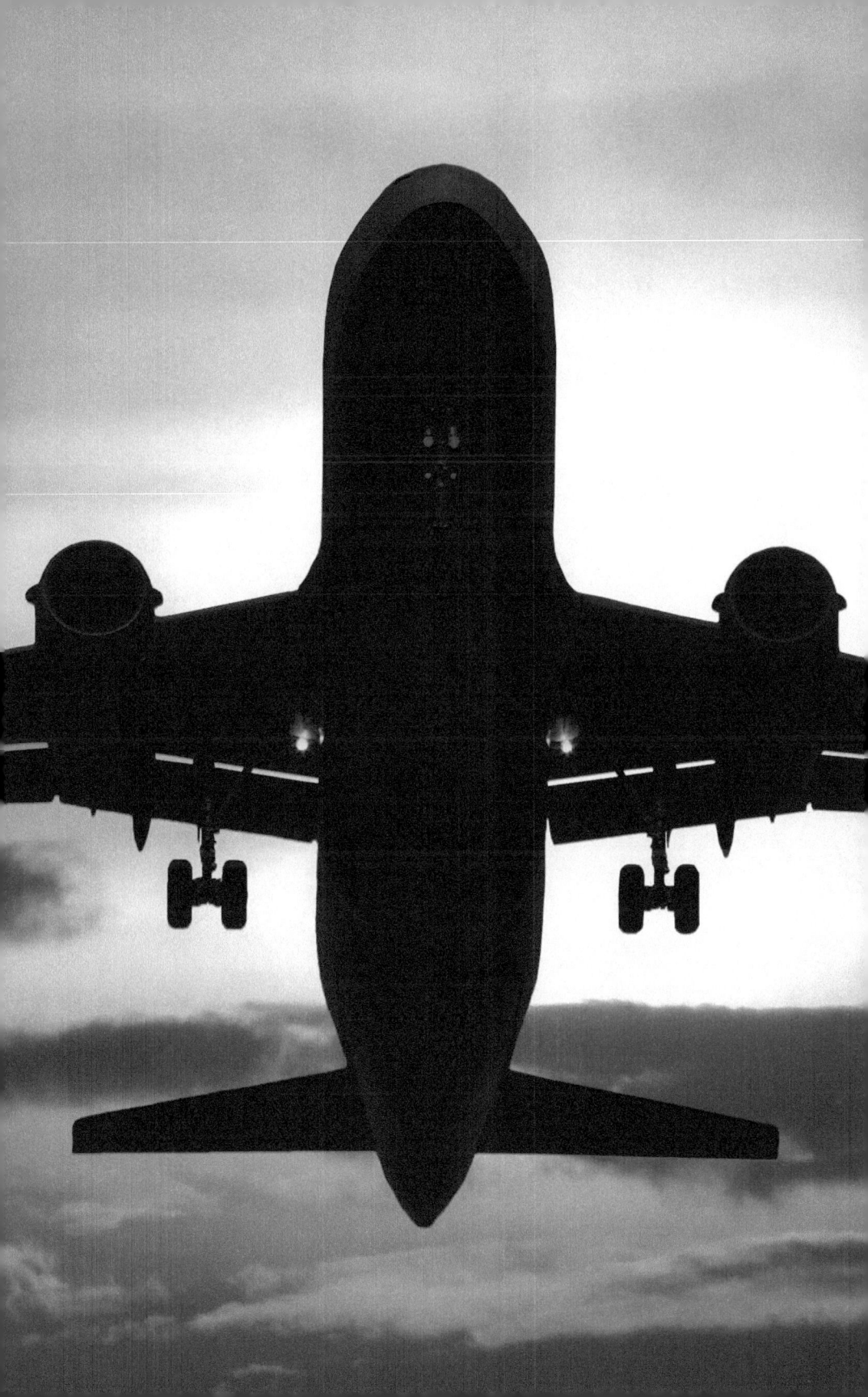

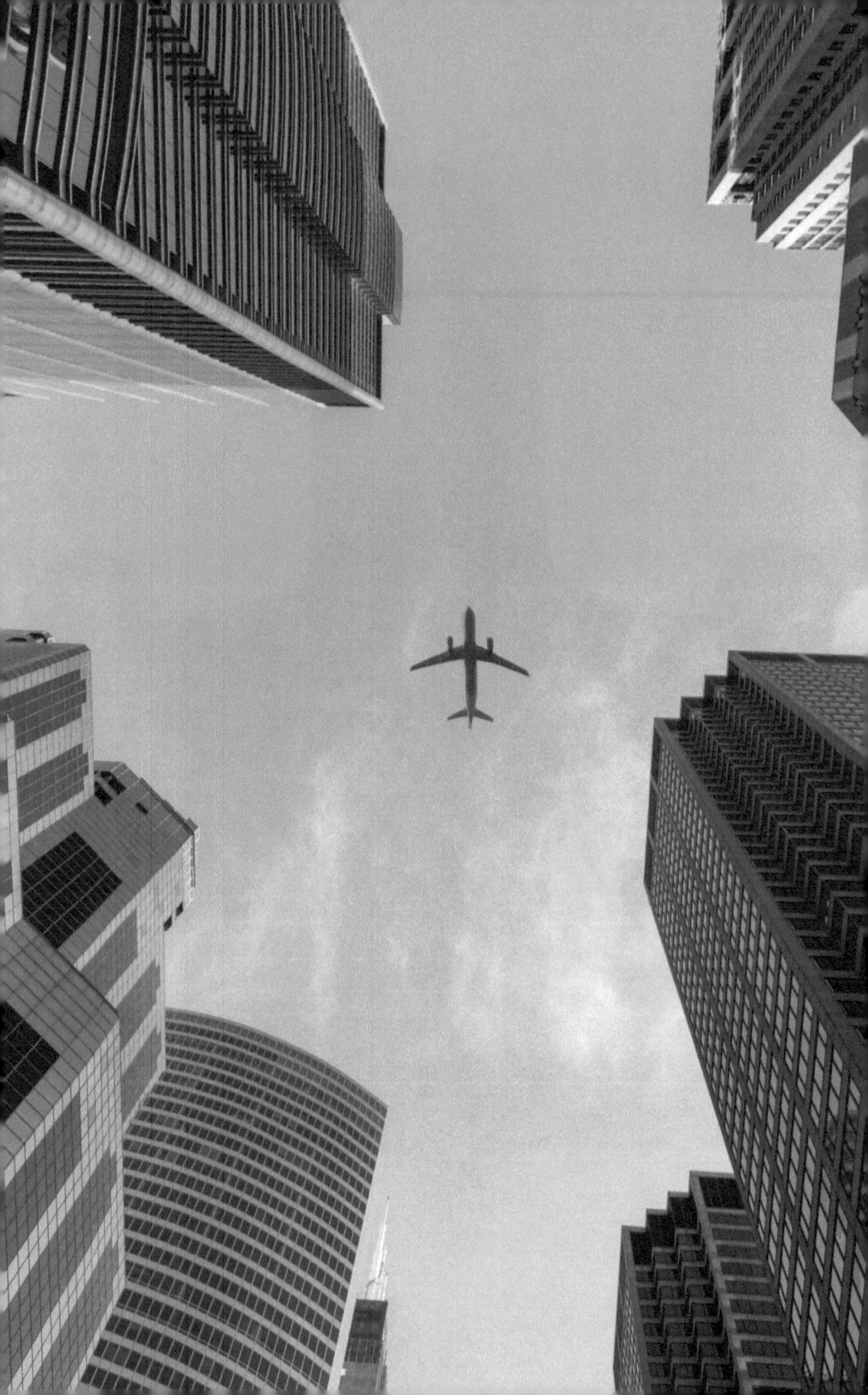

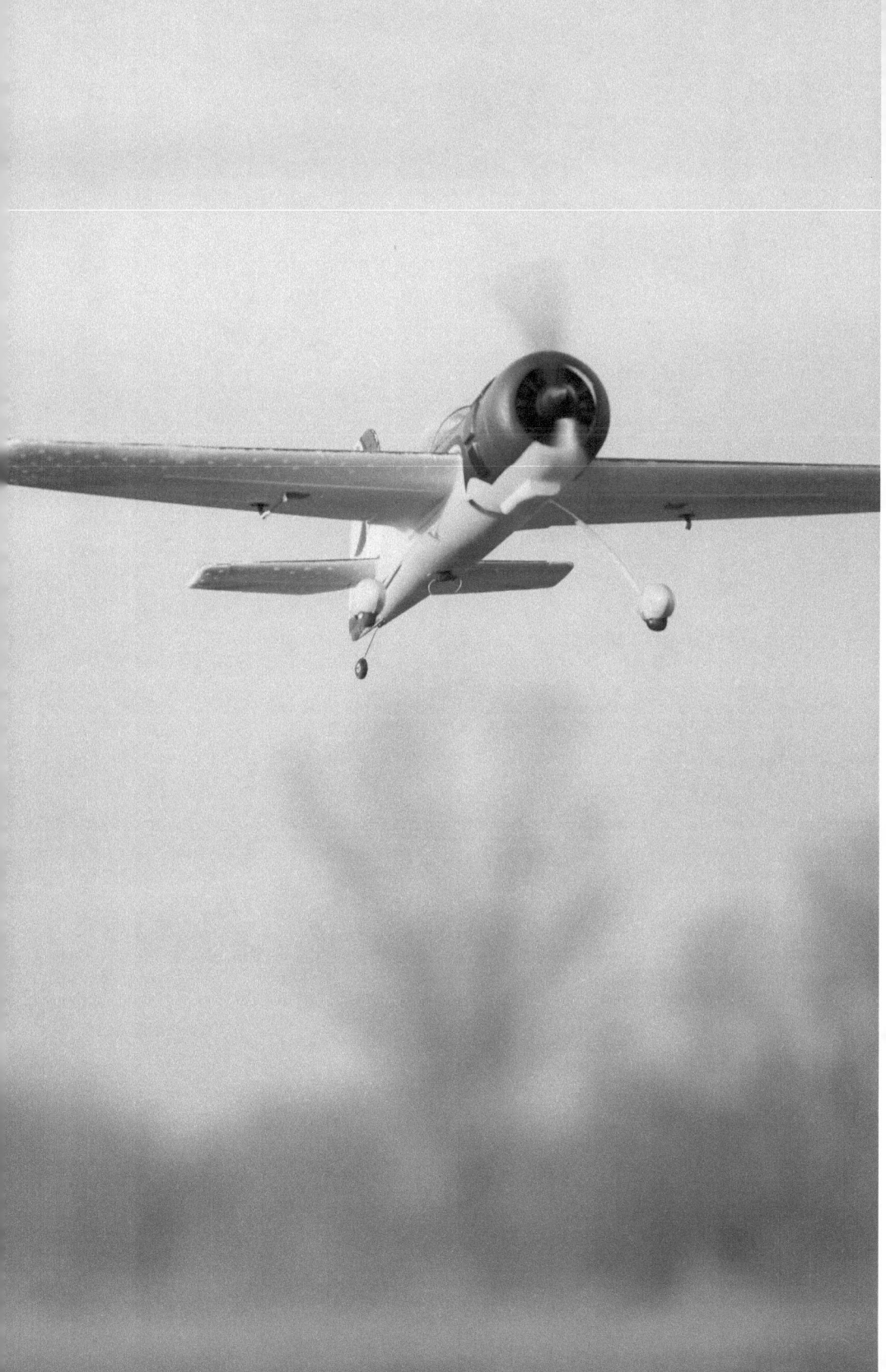

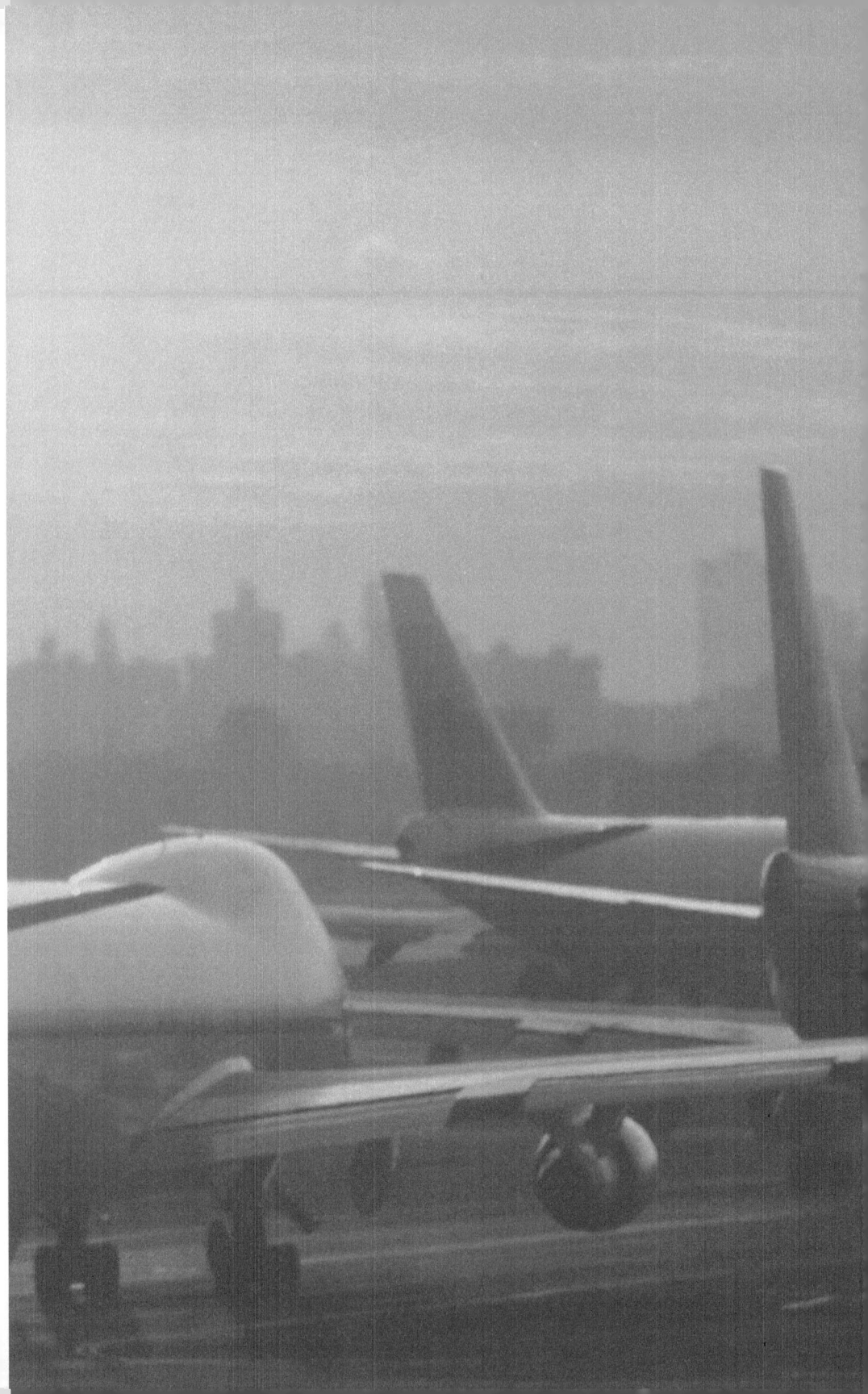

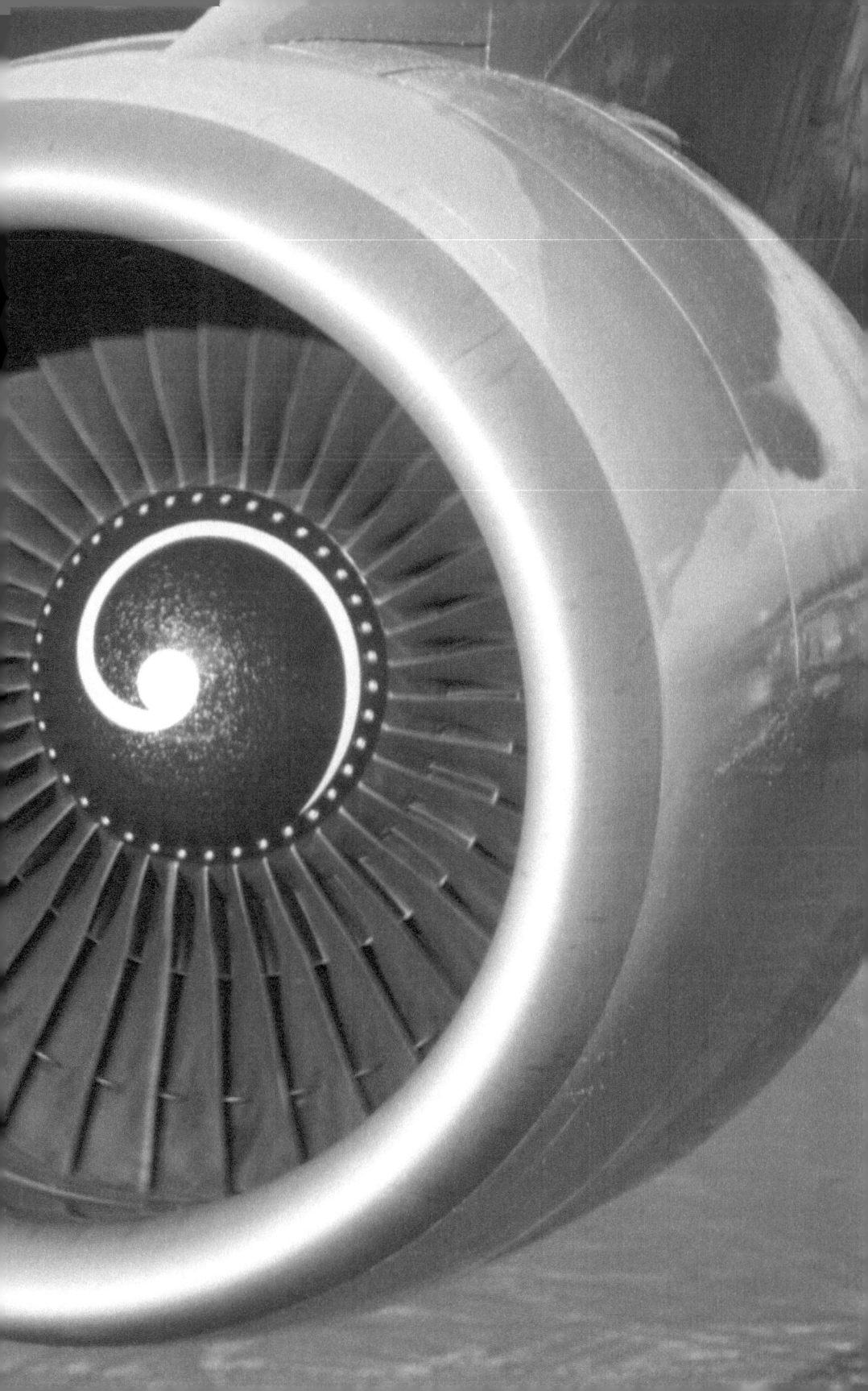

"You wanna fly, you got to give up the shit that weighs you down."

Toni Morrison, Song of Solomon

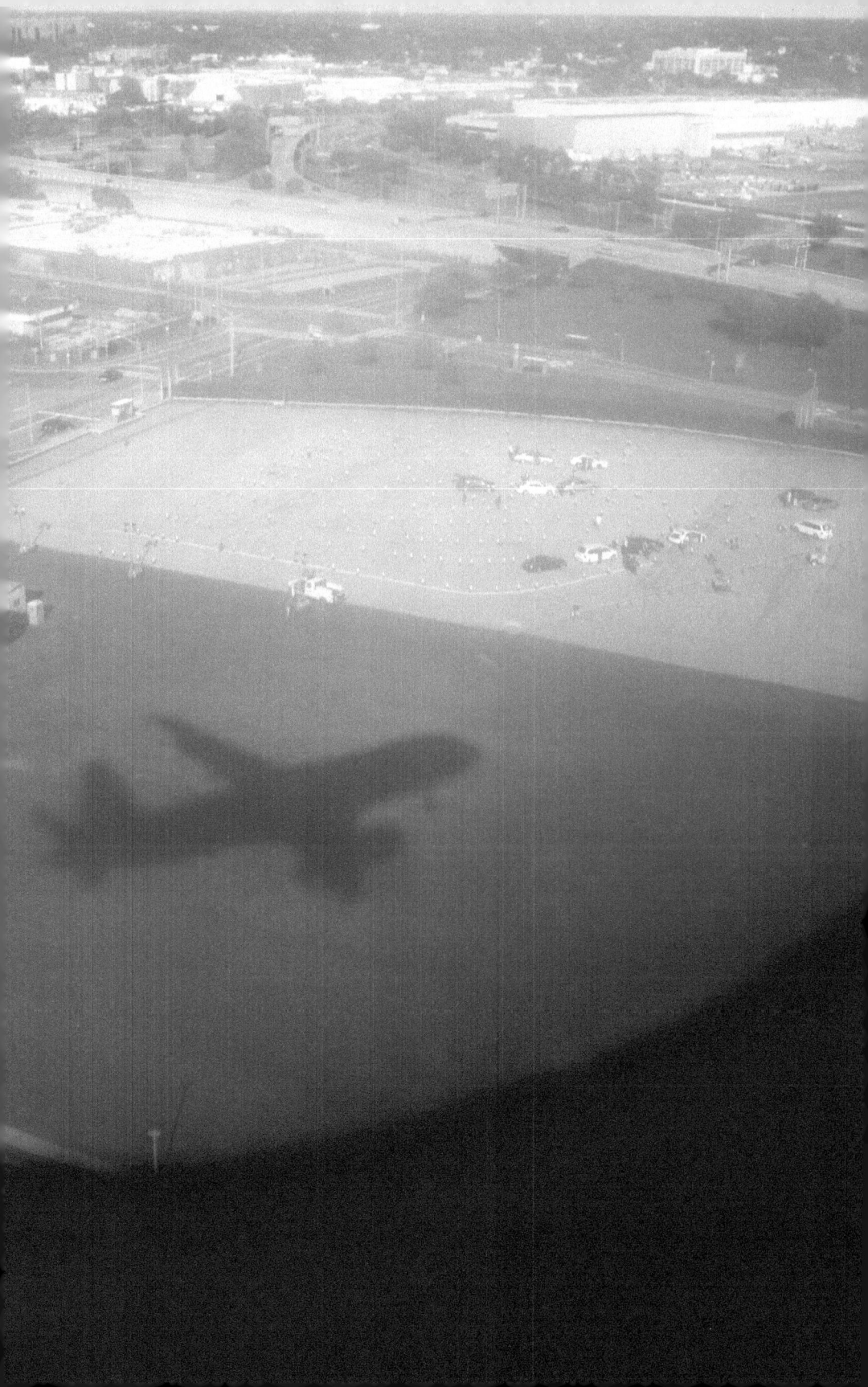

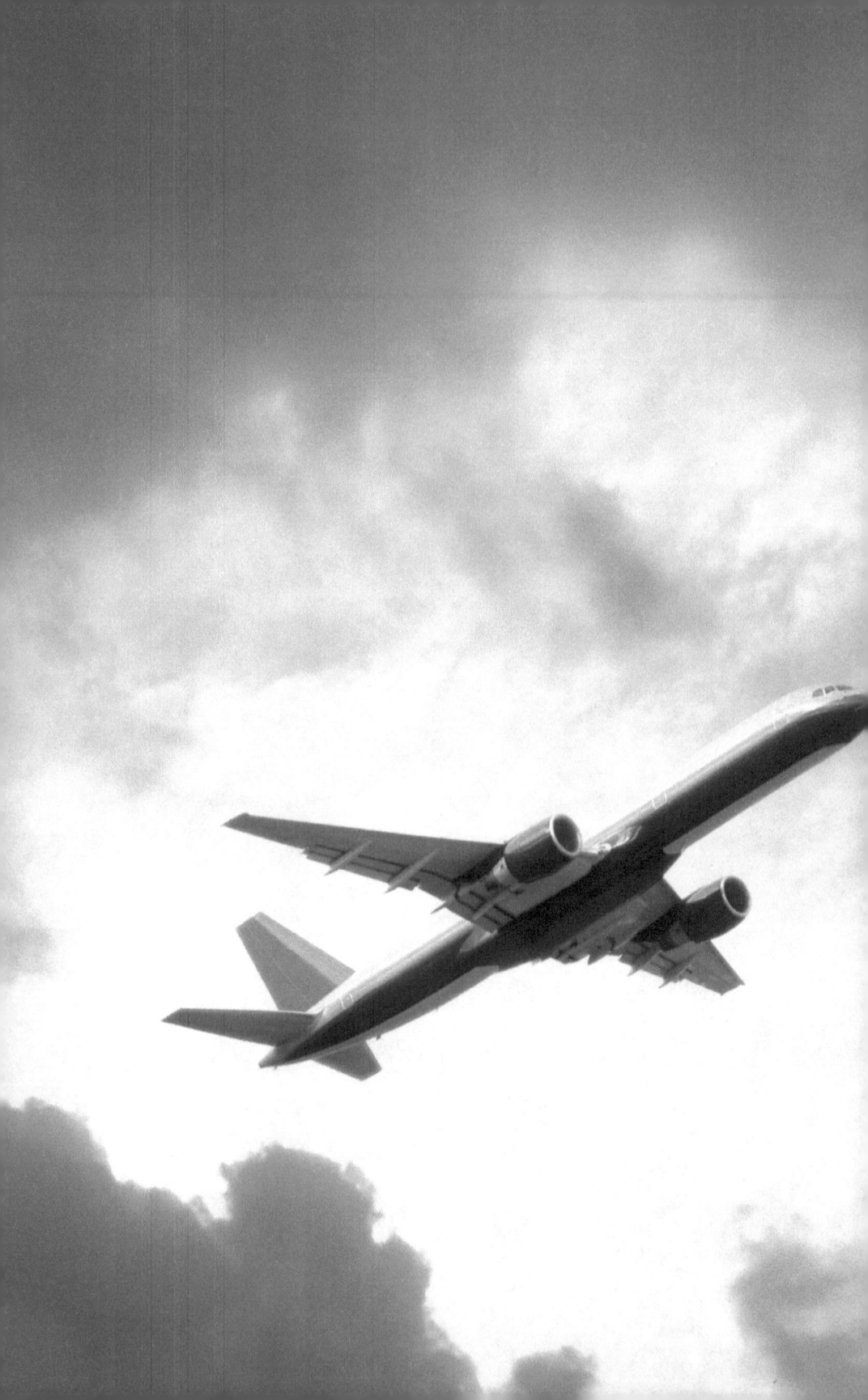

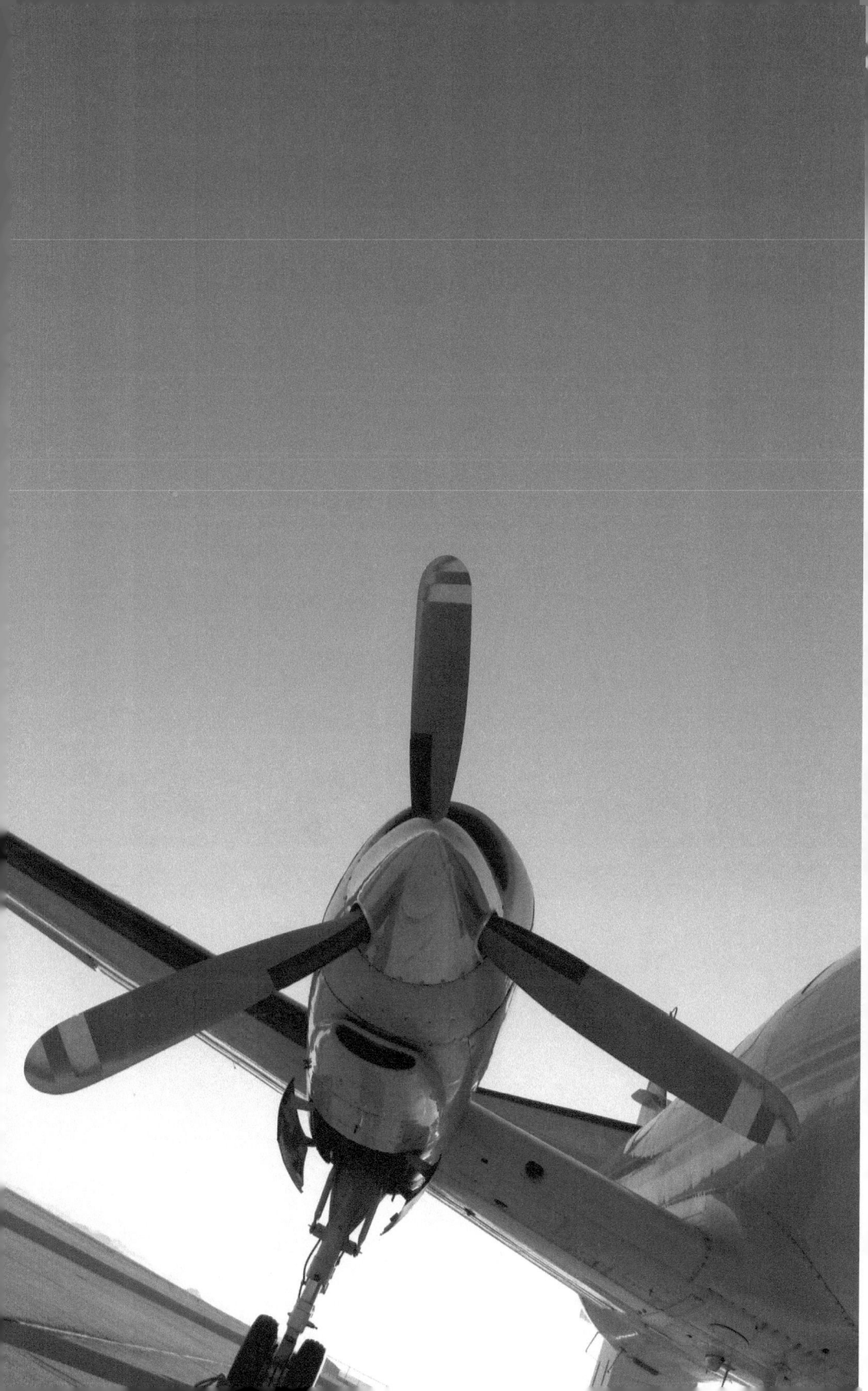

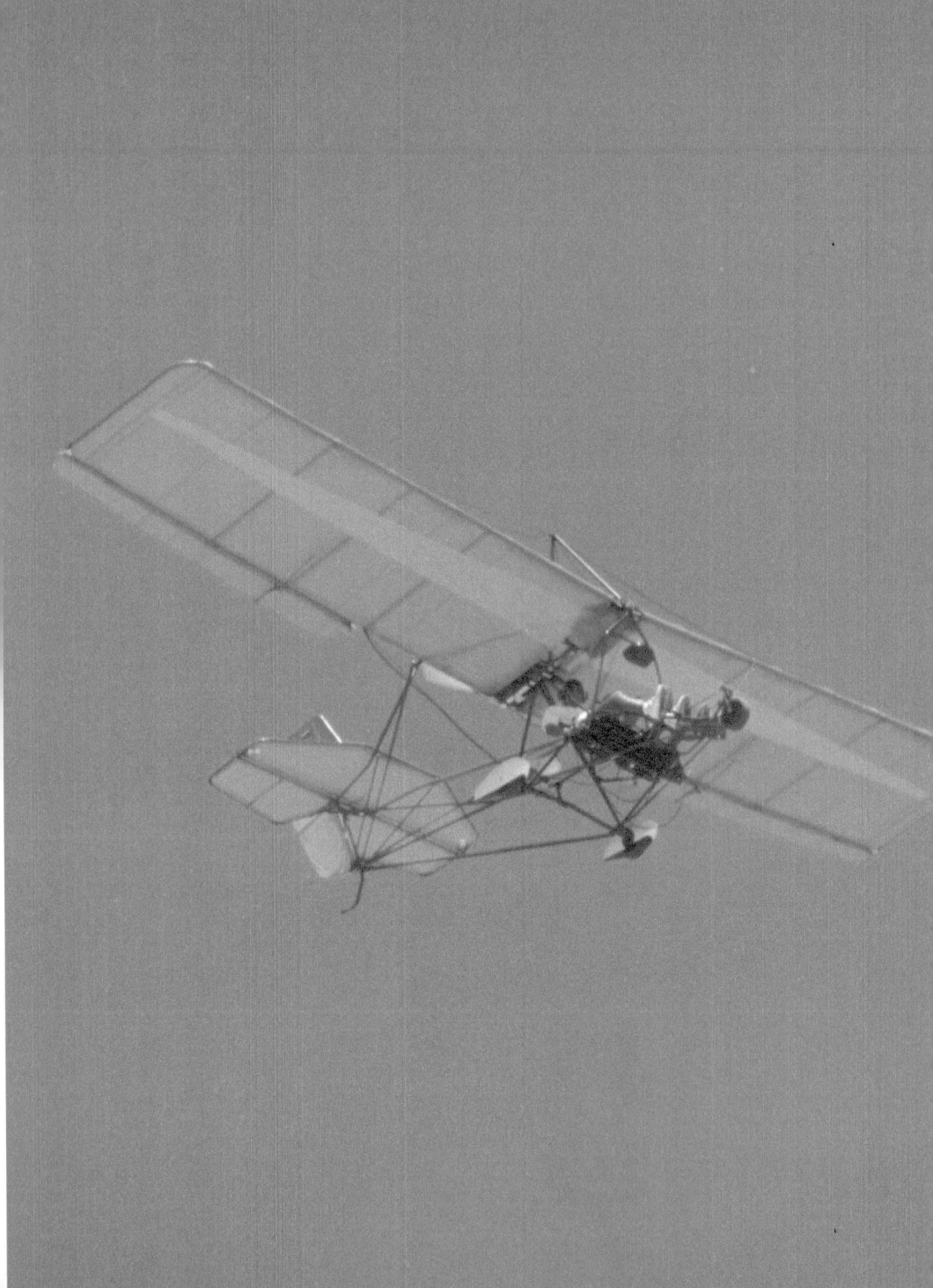

"The reason birds can fly and we can't is simply because they have perfect faith, for to have faith is to have wings."

J.M. Barrie, The Little White Bird

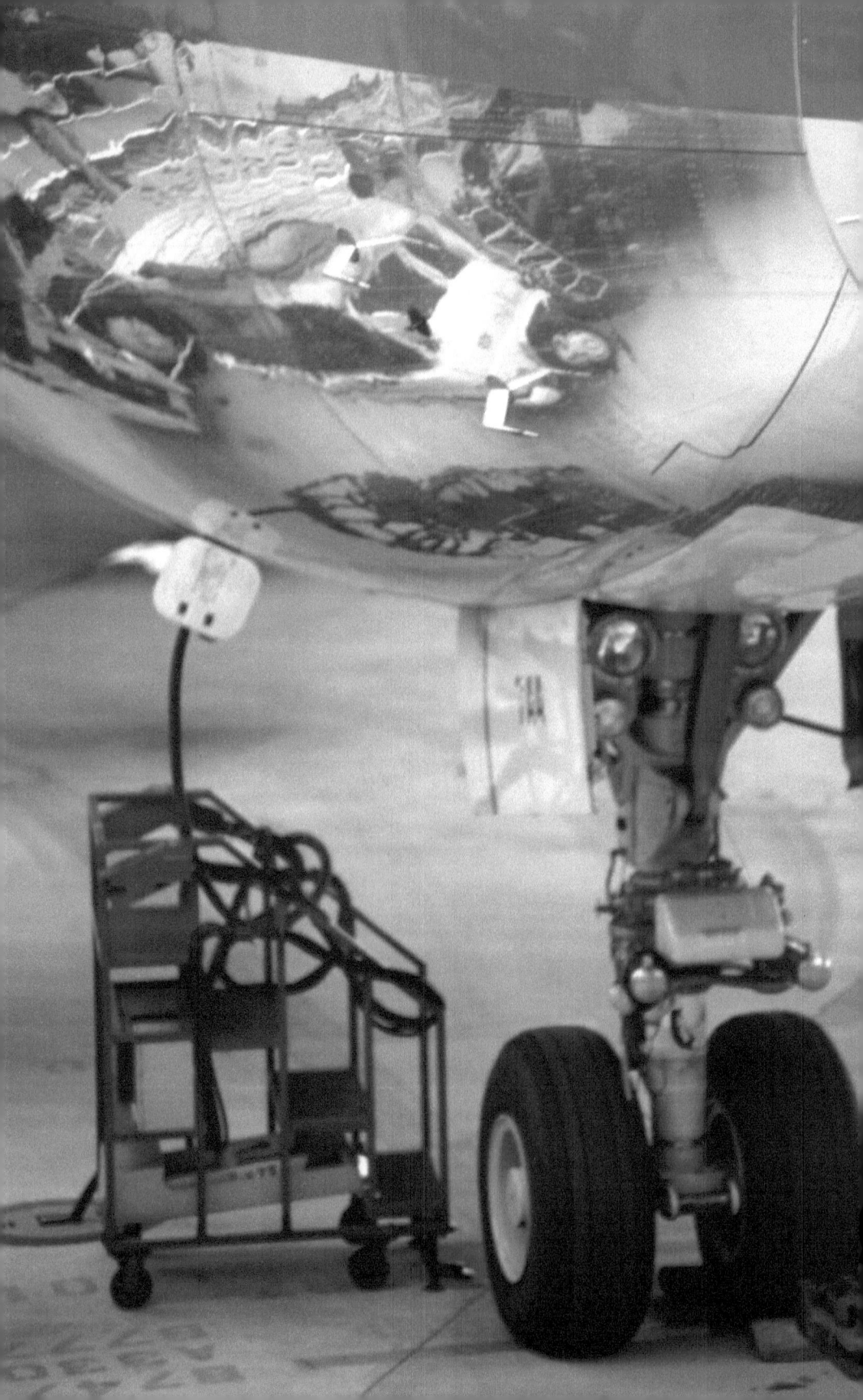

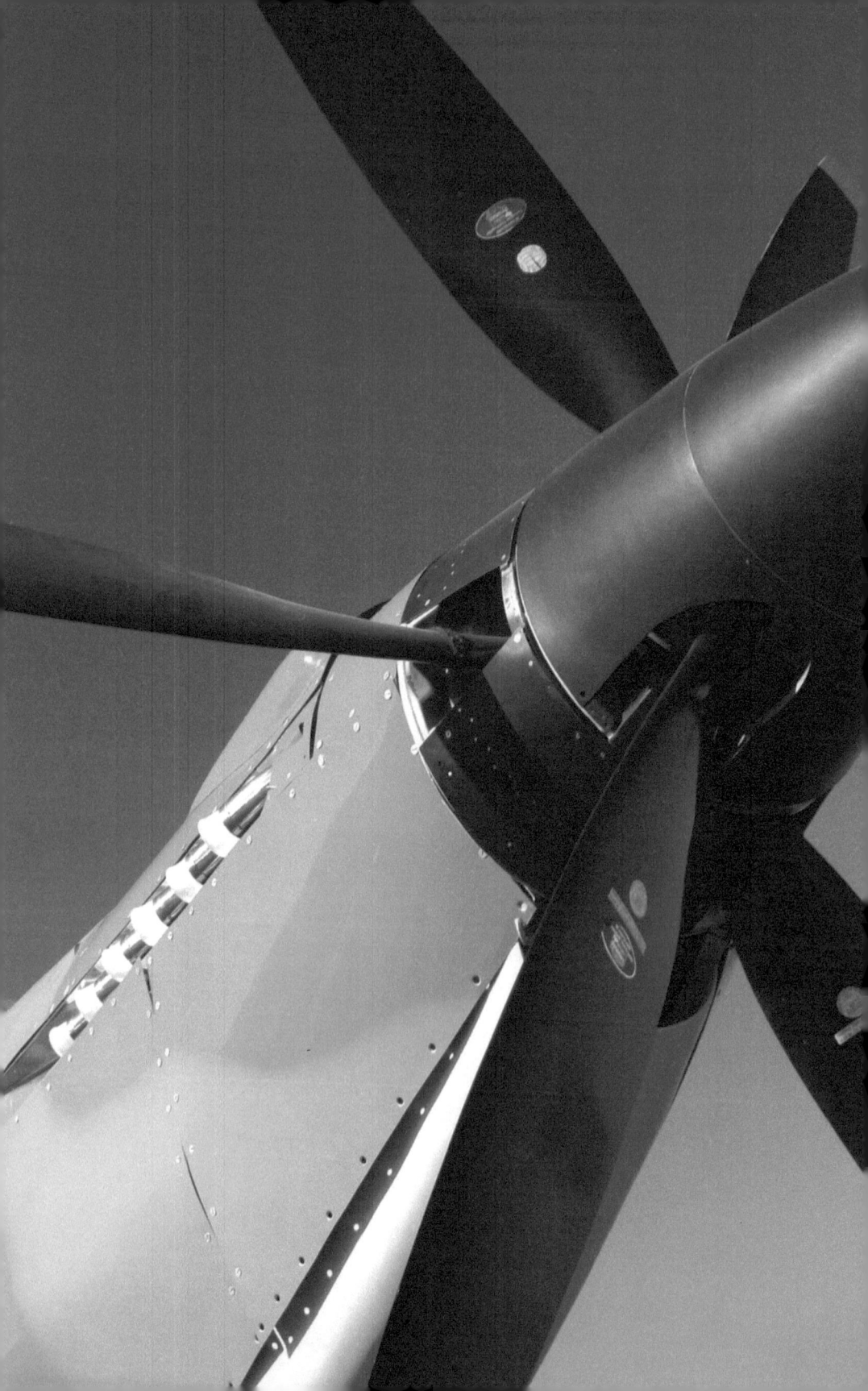

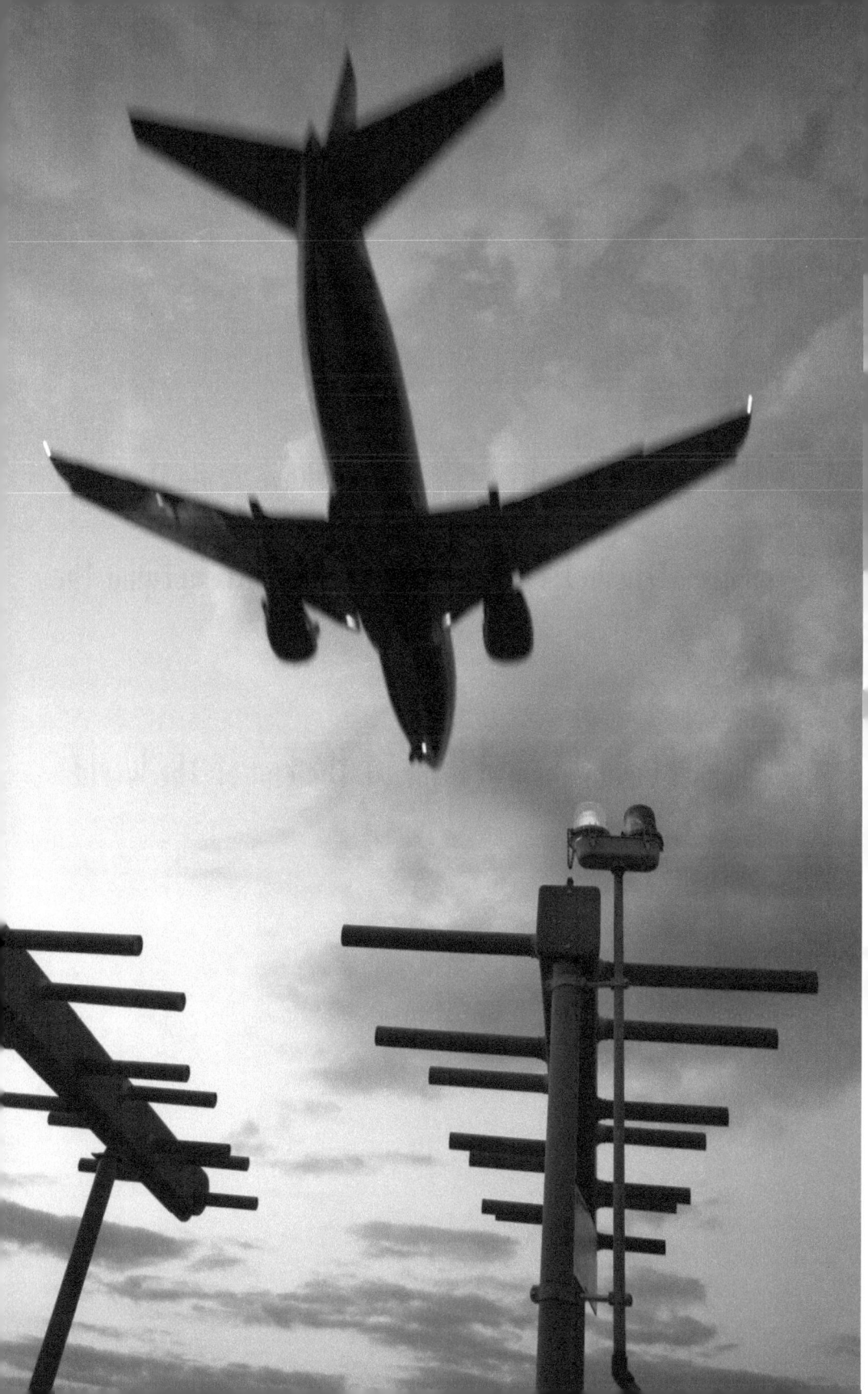

"The secret of flight is this -- you have to do it immediately, before your body realizes it is defying the laws."

Michael Cunningham, A Home at the End of the World

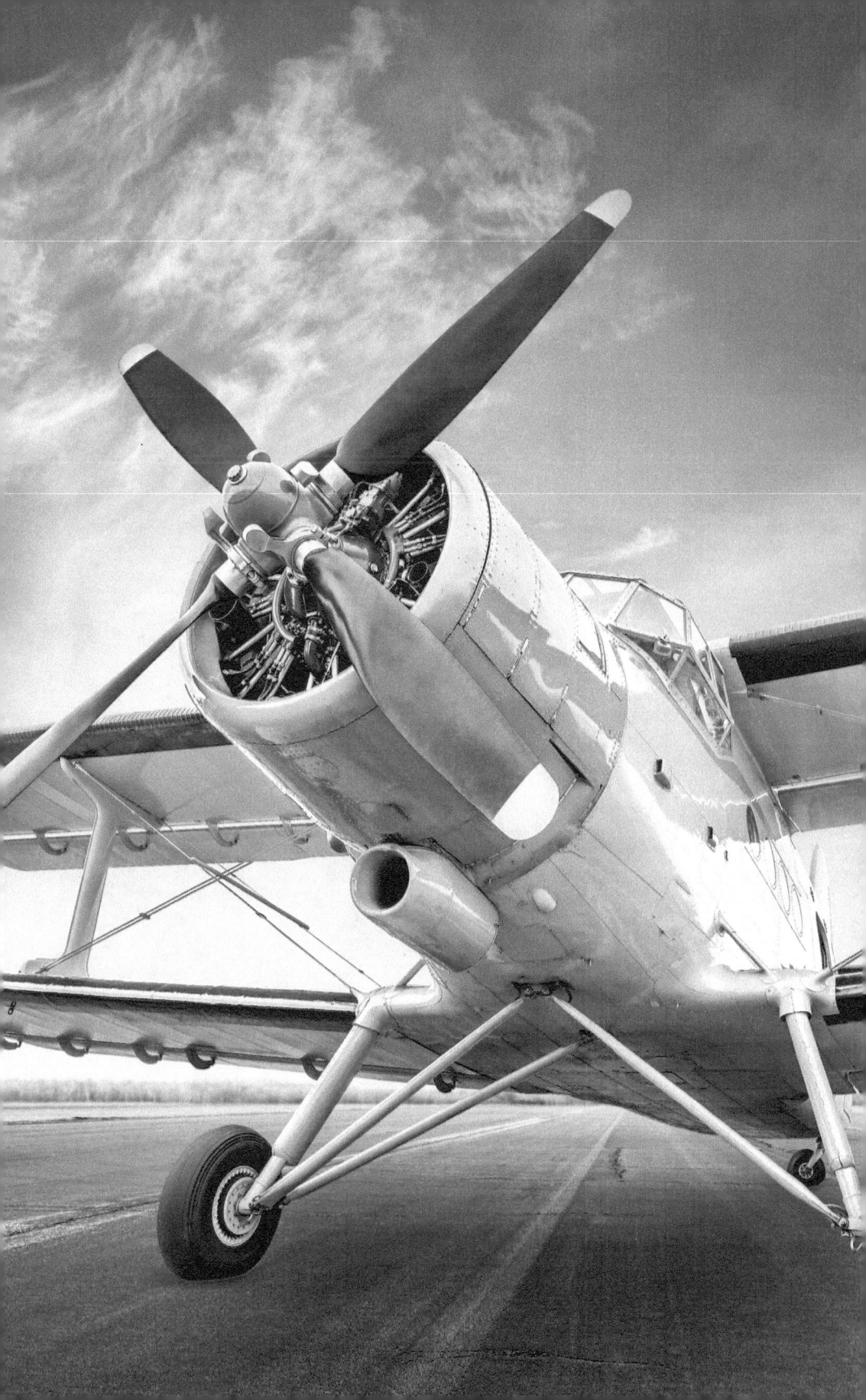

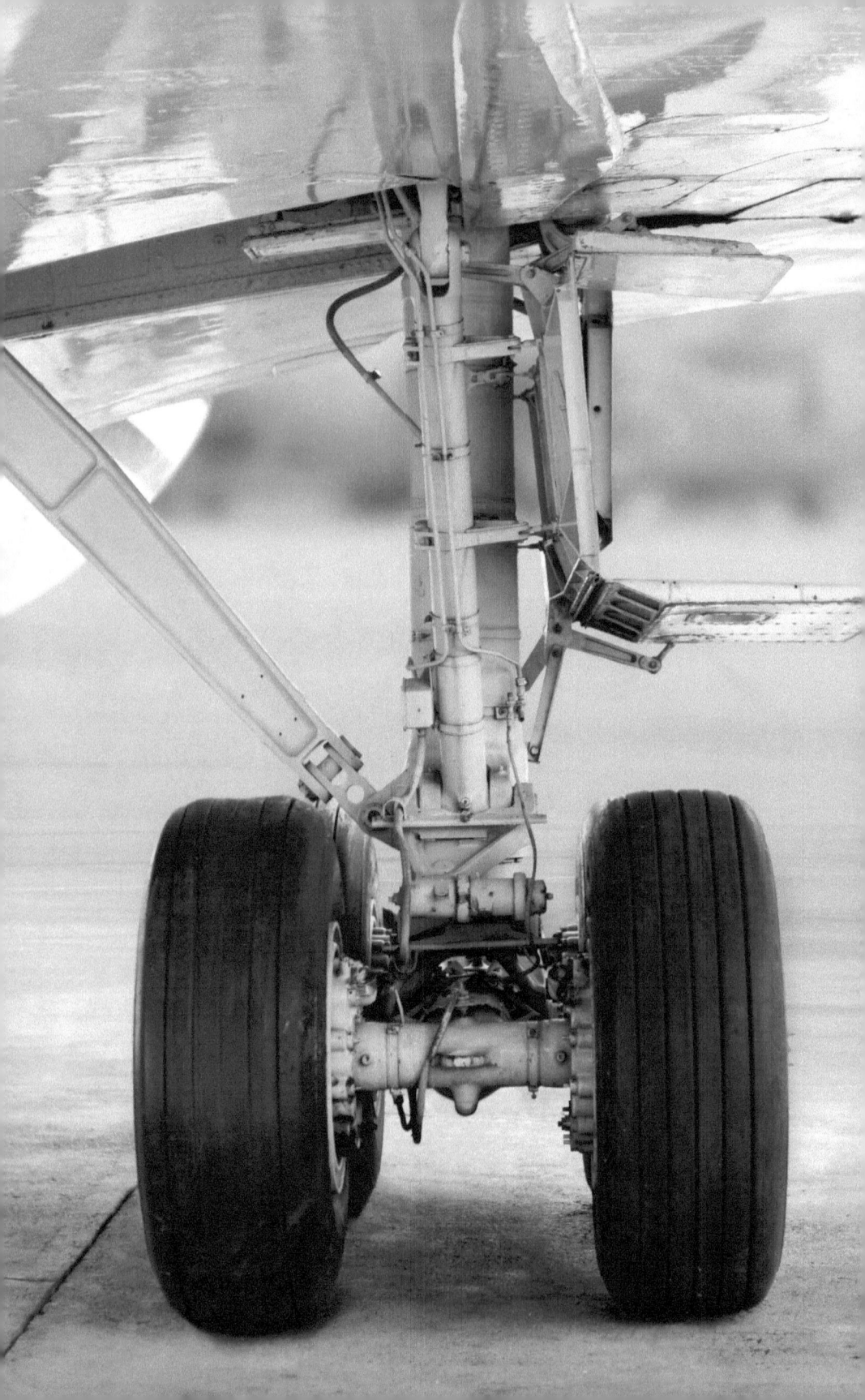

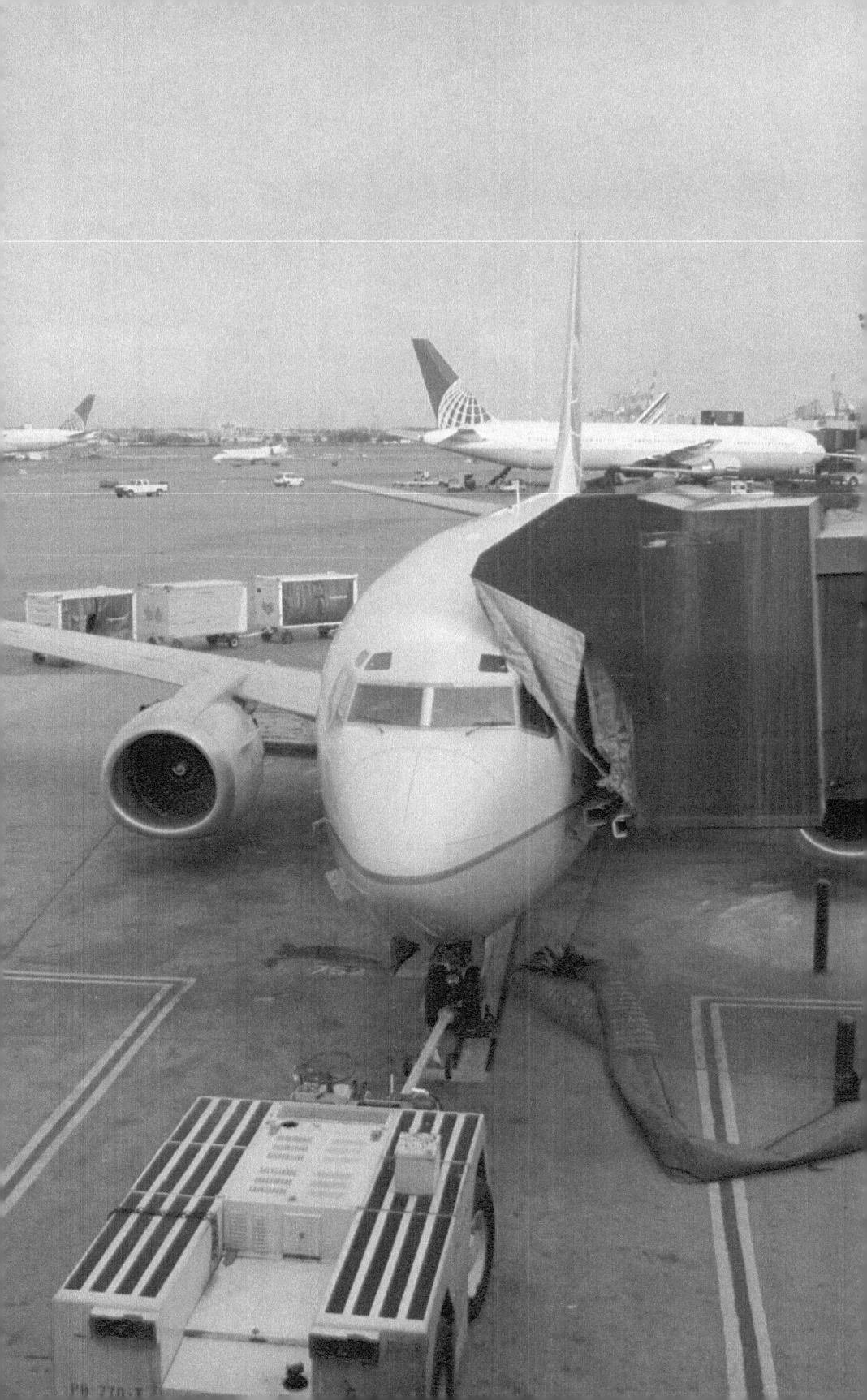

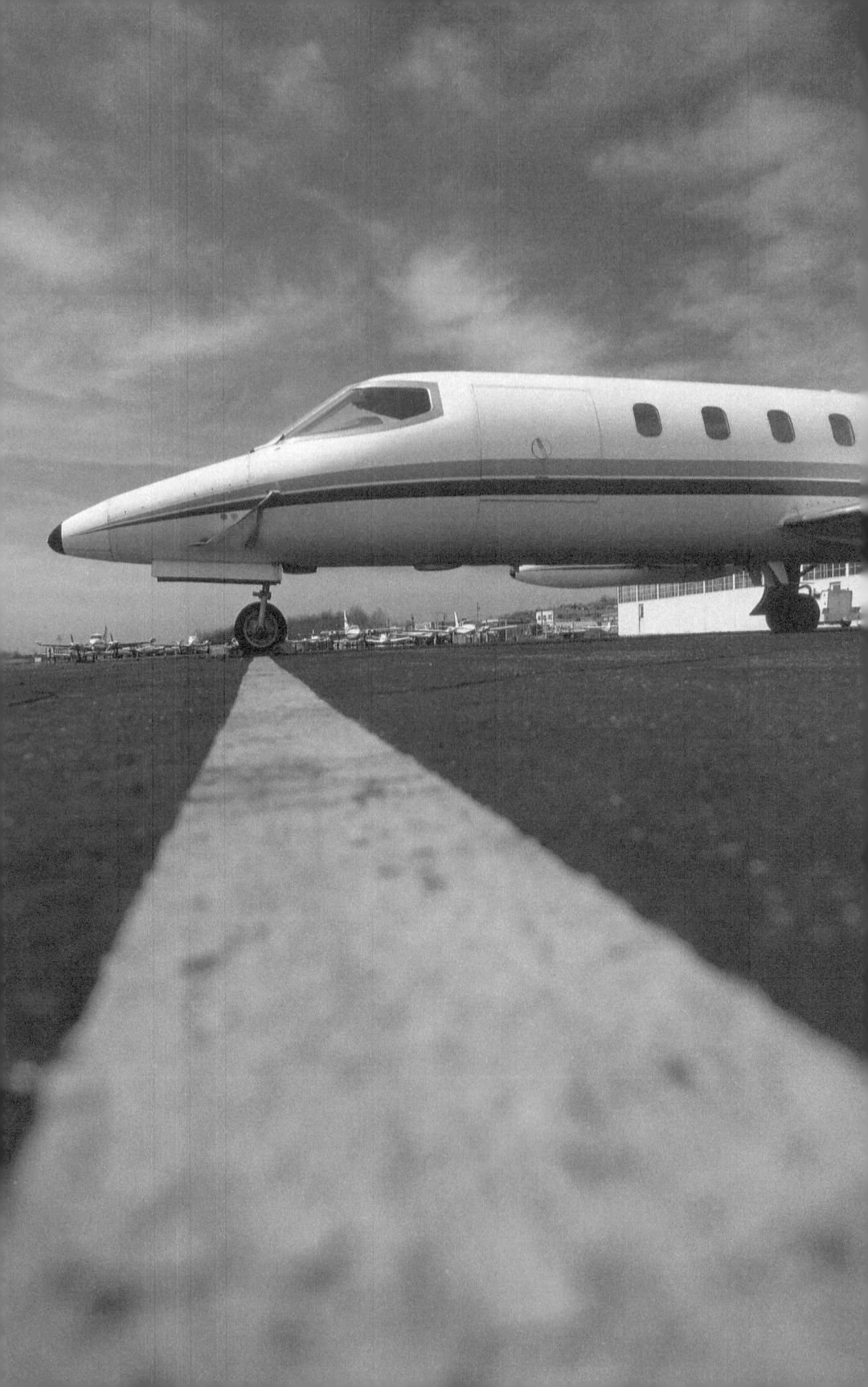

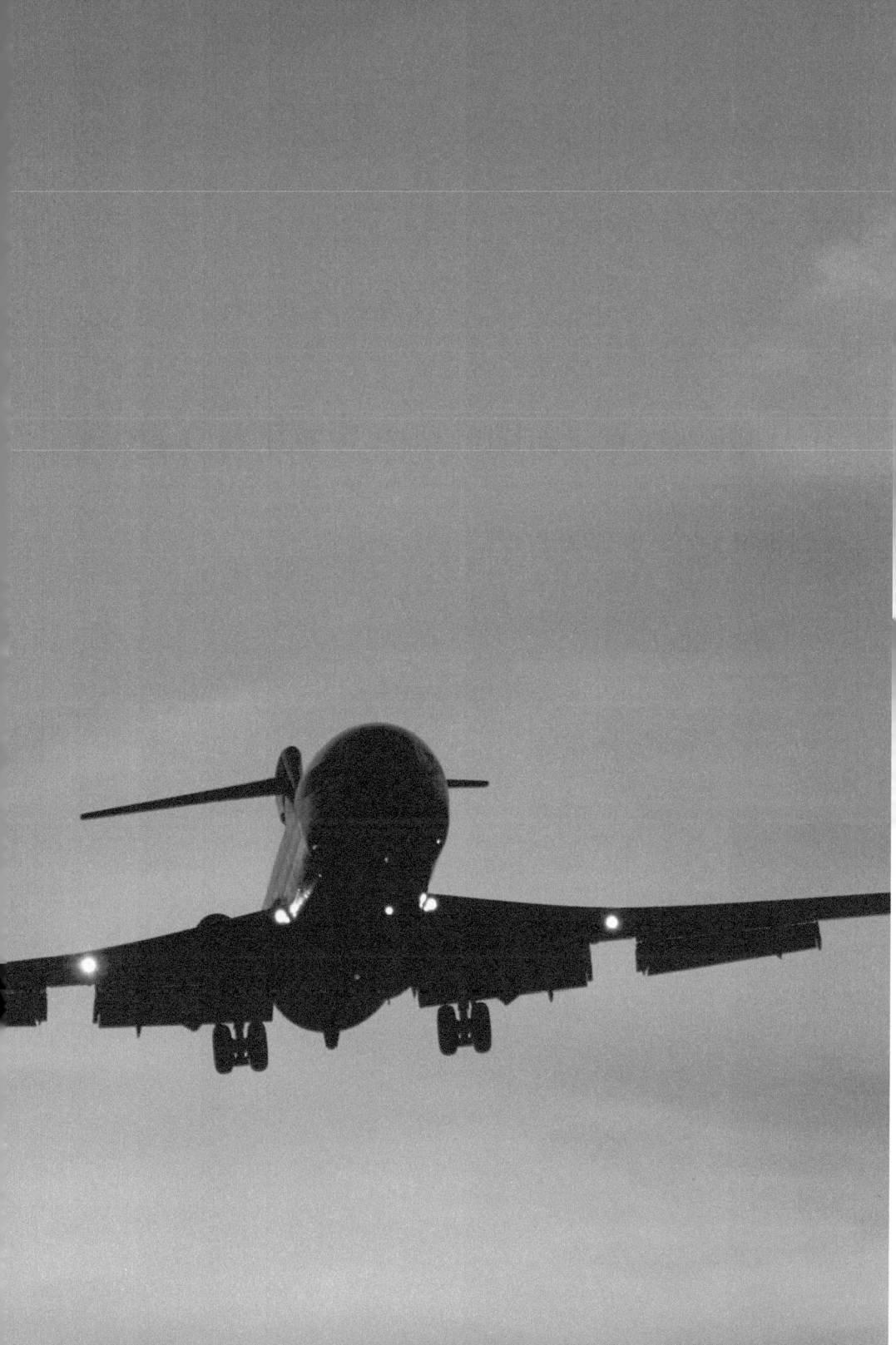

"If you were born without wings, do nothing to prevent them from growing."

Coco Chanel

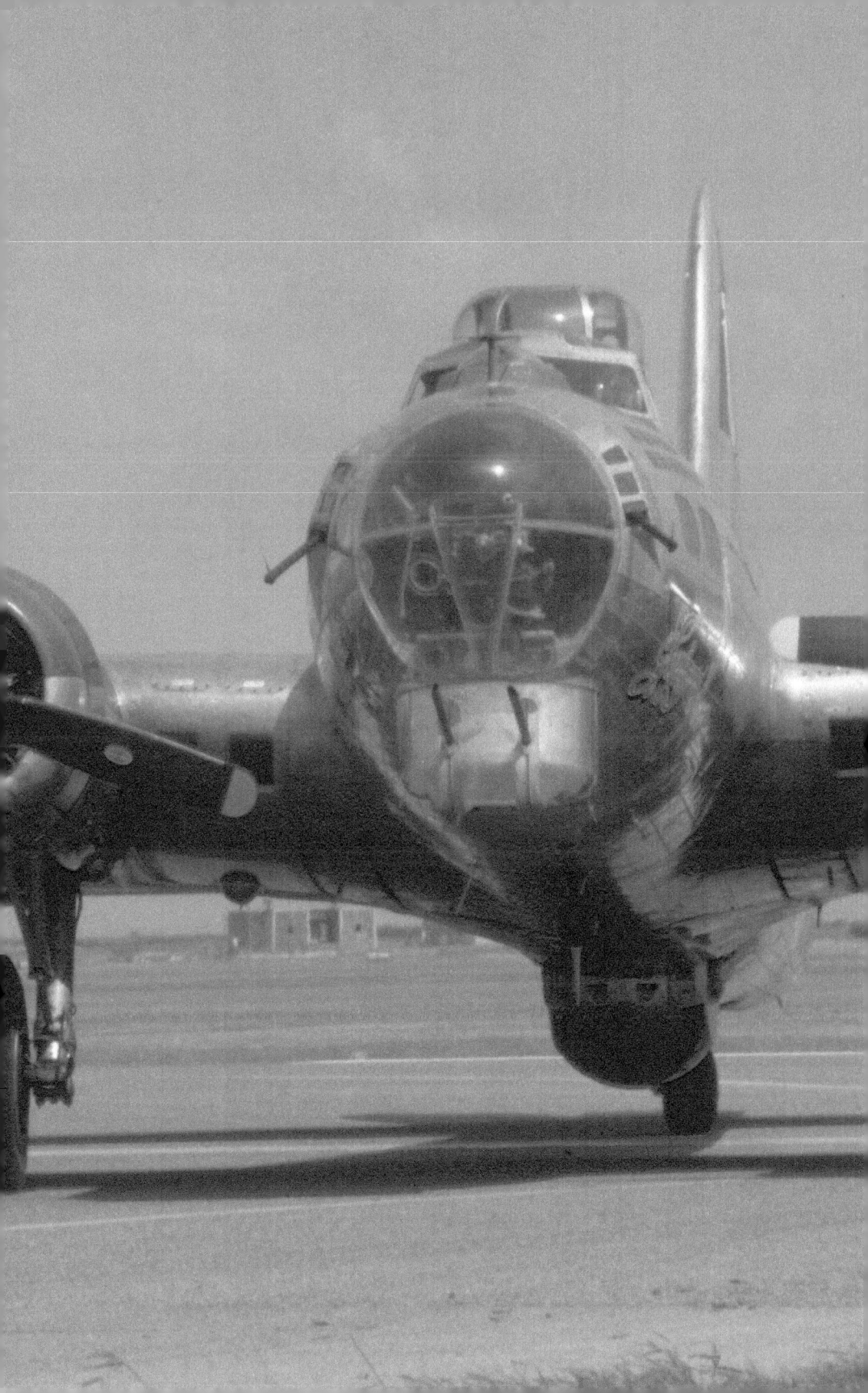

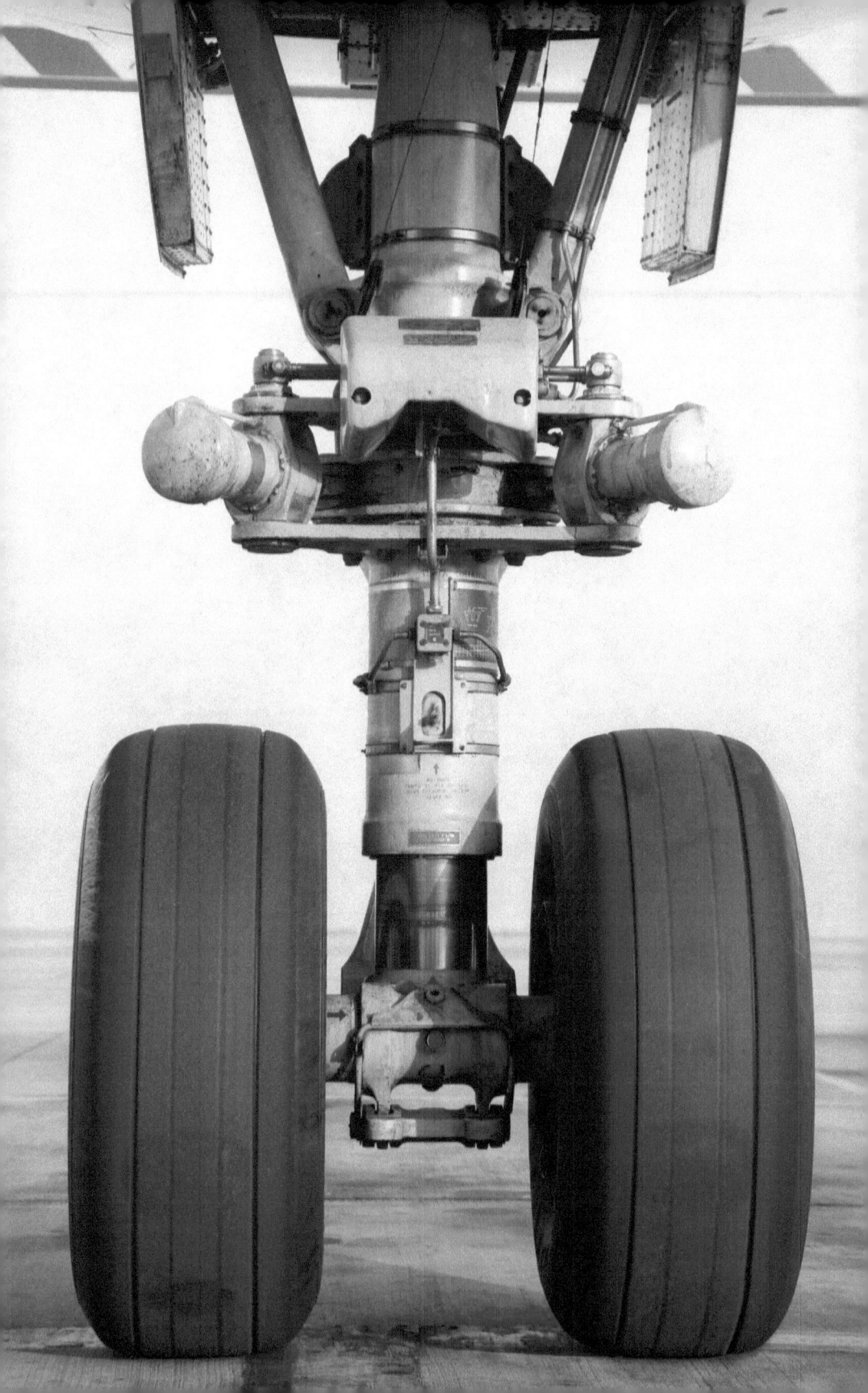

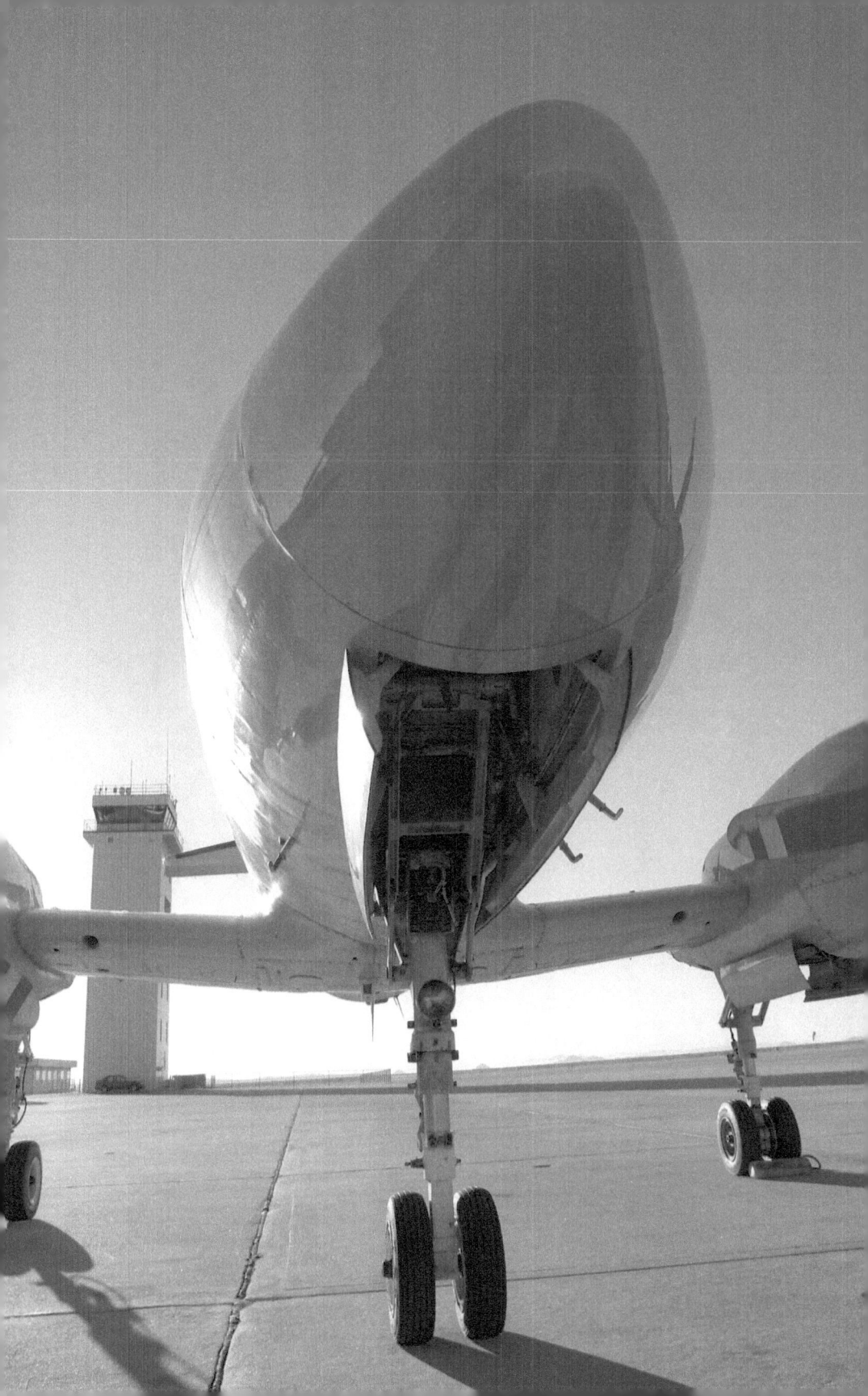

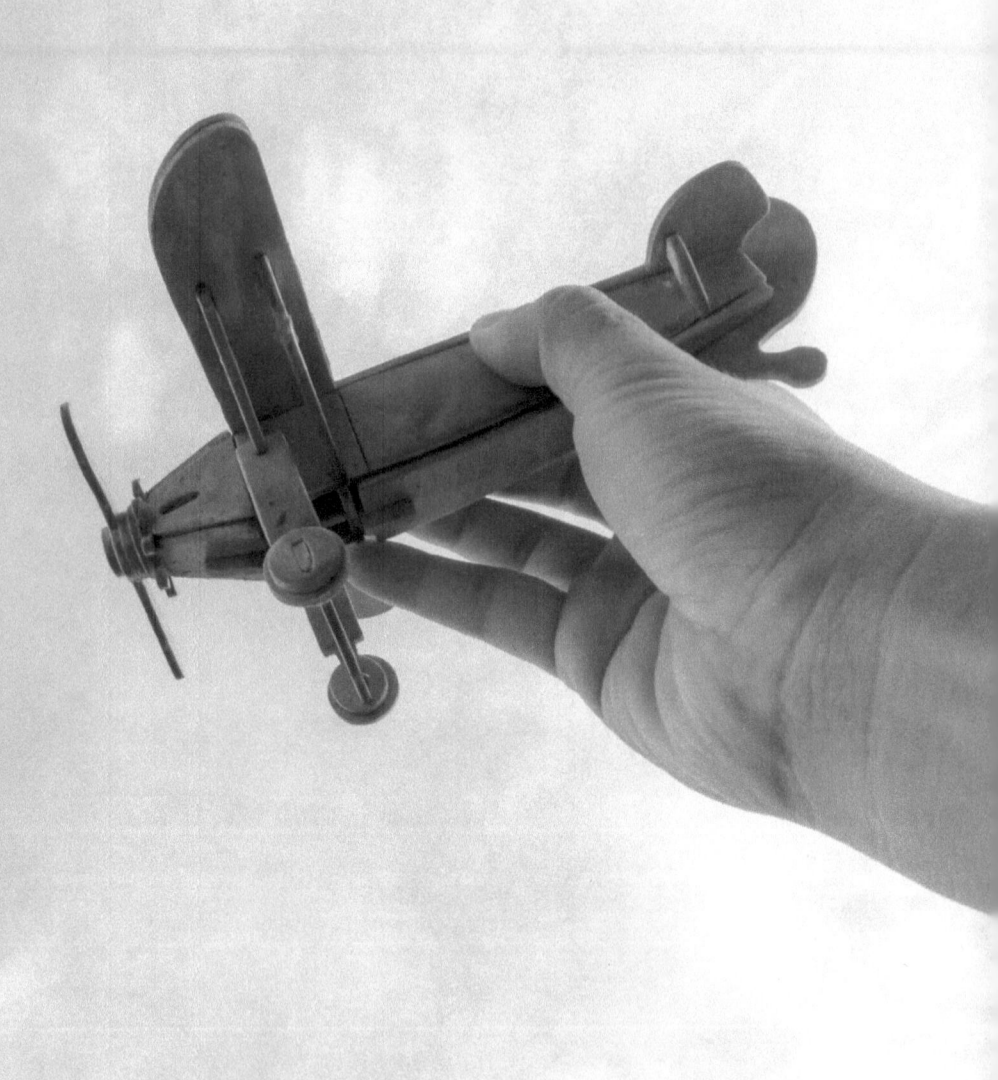

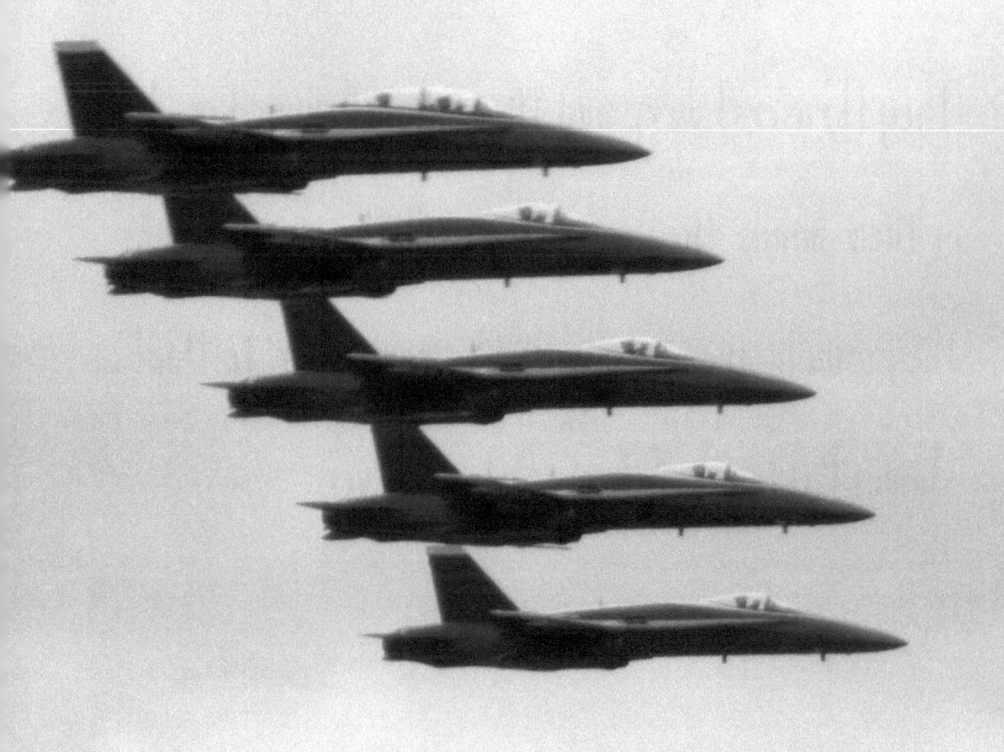

"They [Erasers] were bad fliers," Angel chimed in, "And in their minds, they weren't all kill the mutants, like they usually are. They were like, remember to flap!"

James Patterson, School's Out—Forever

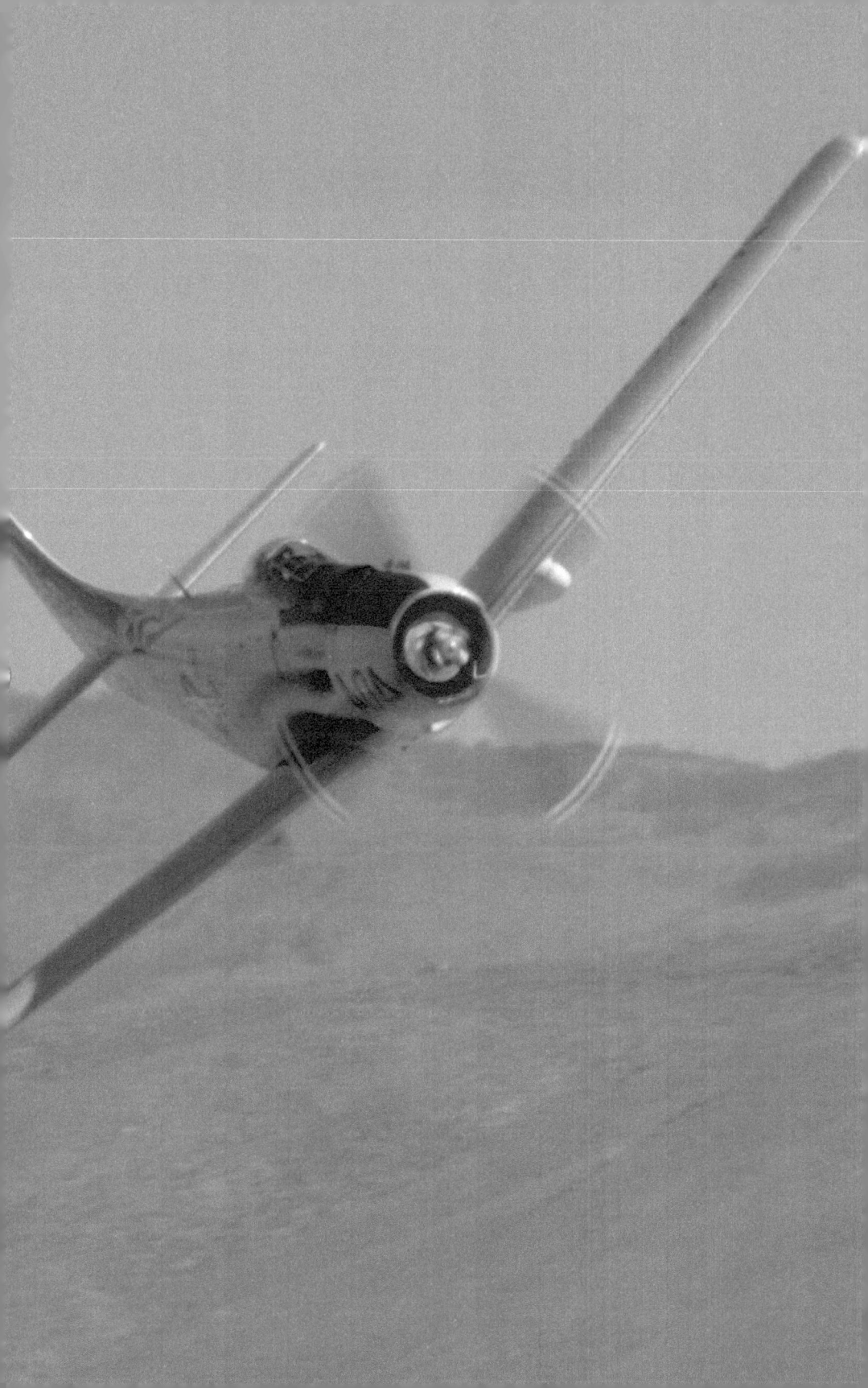

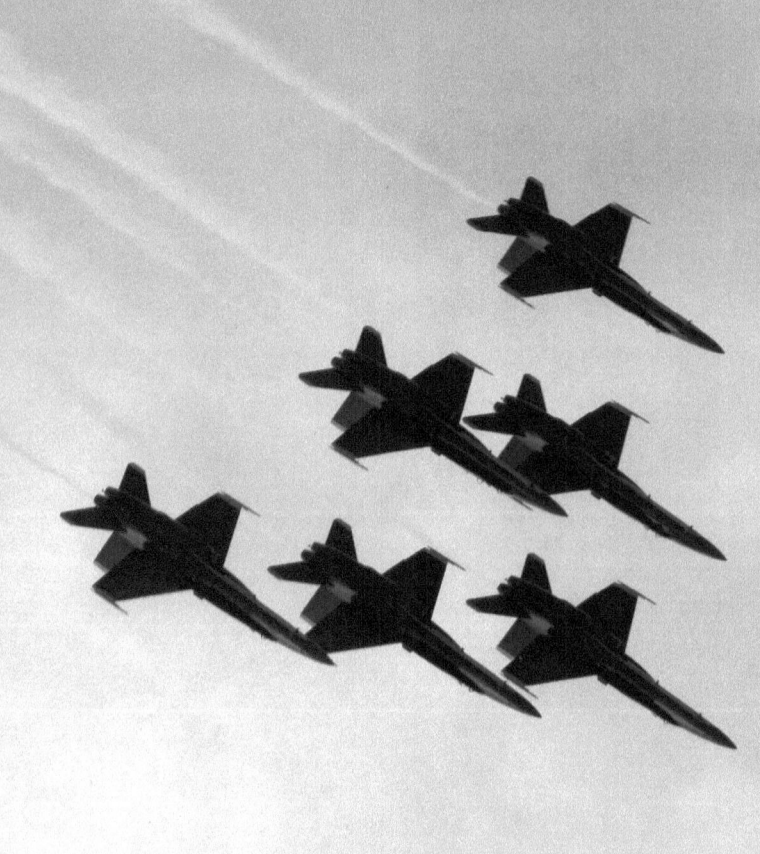

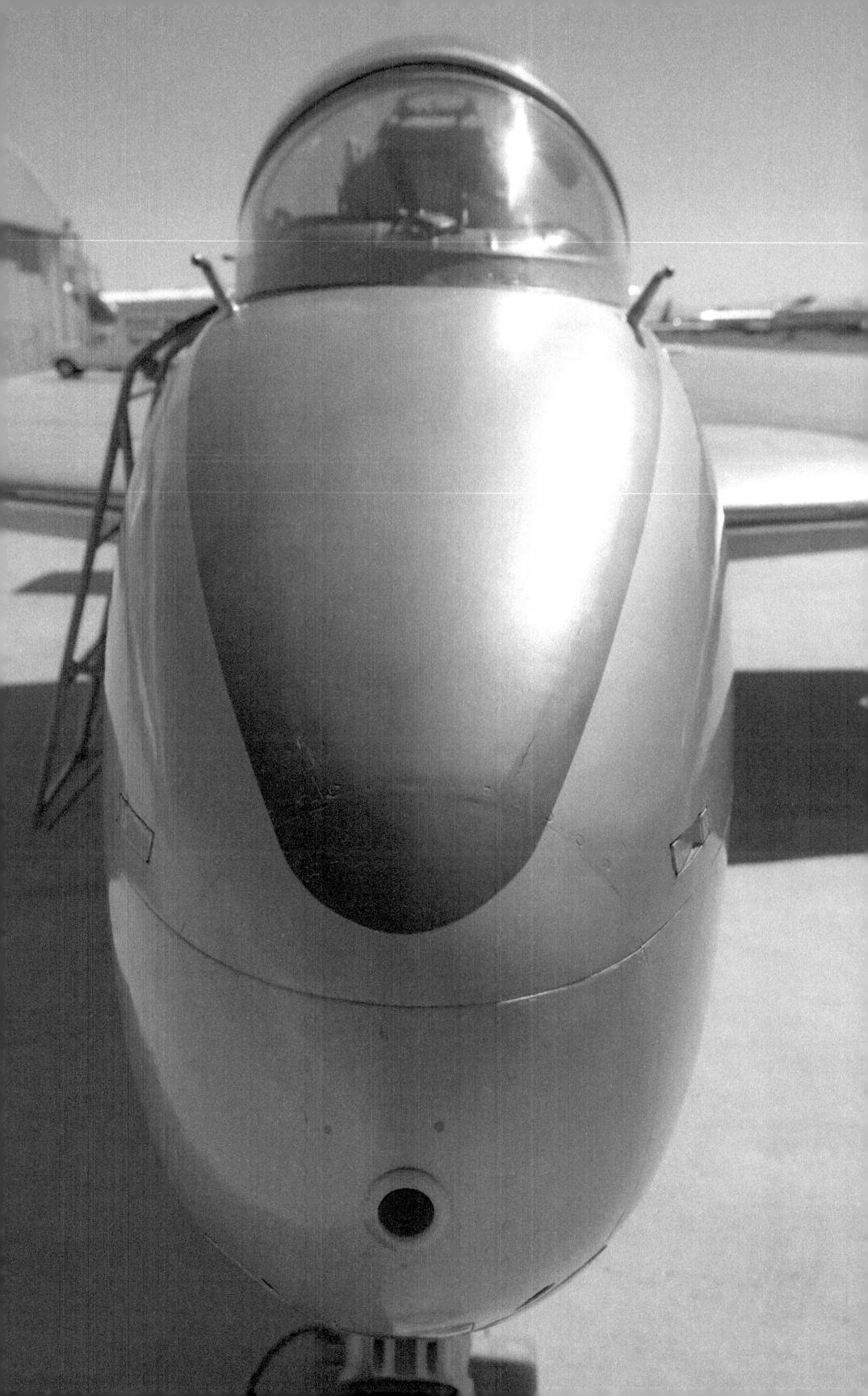

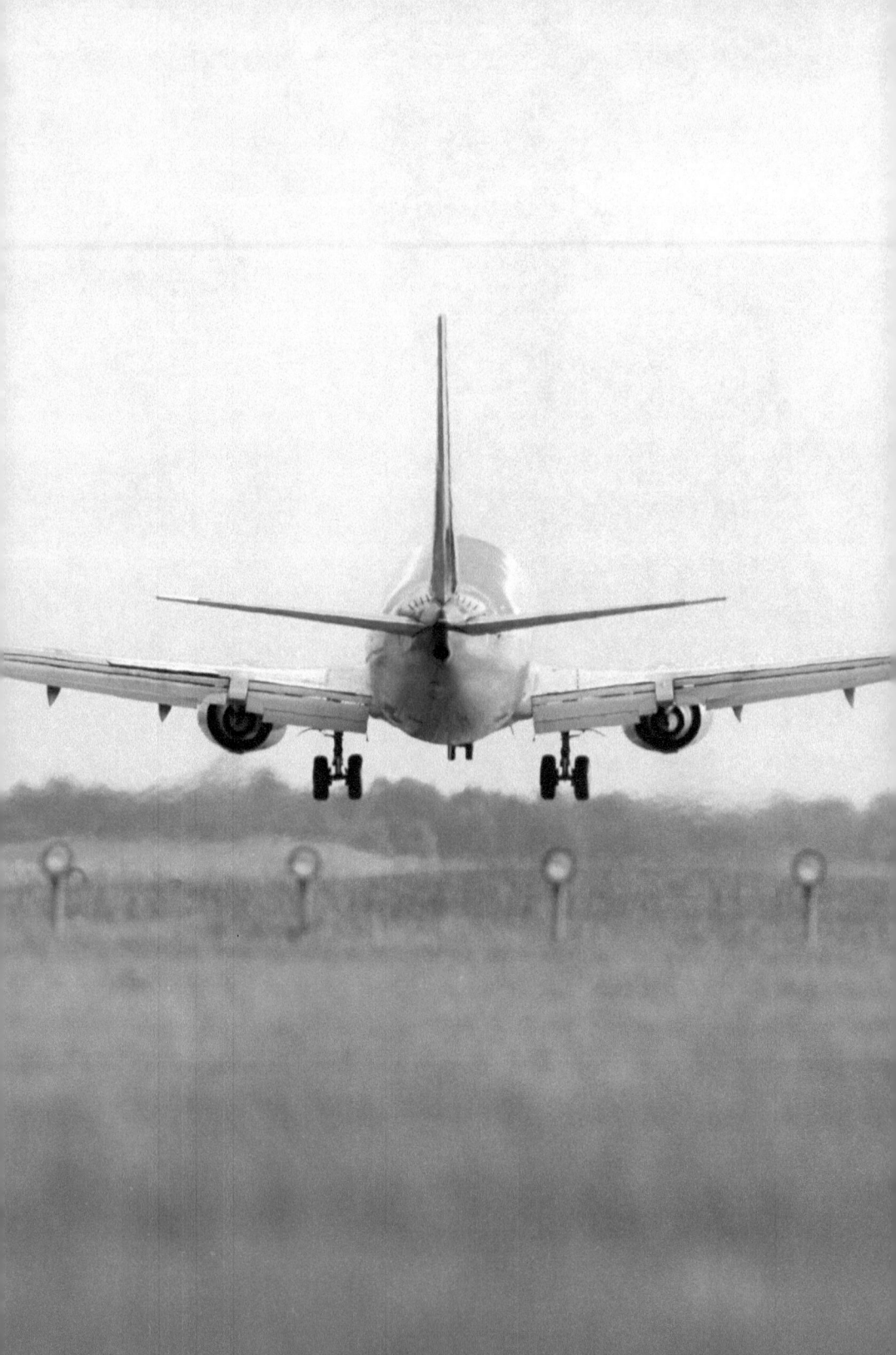

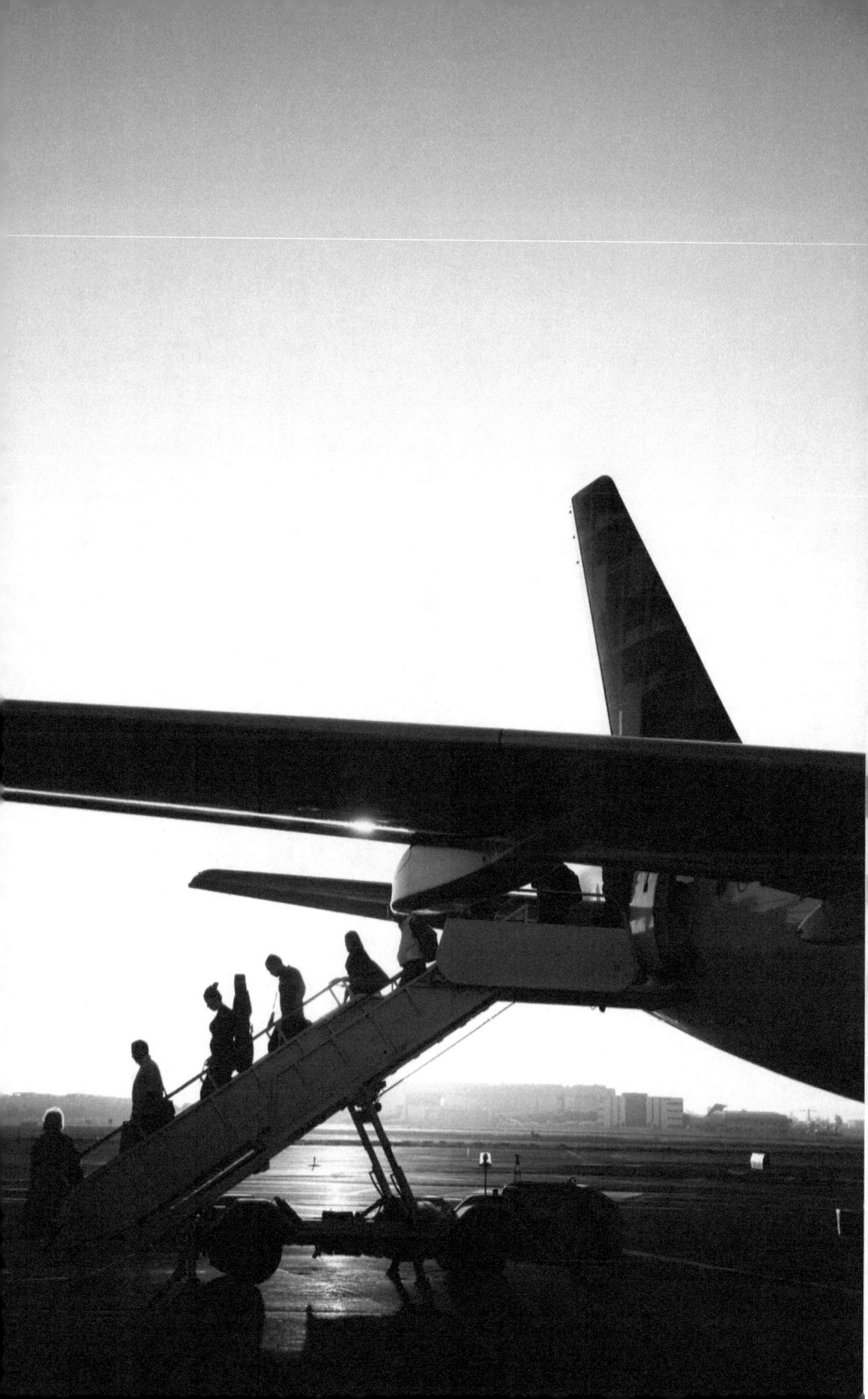

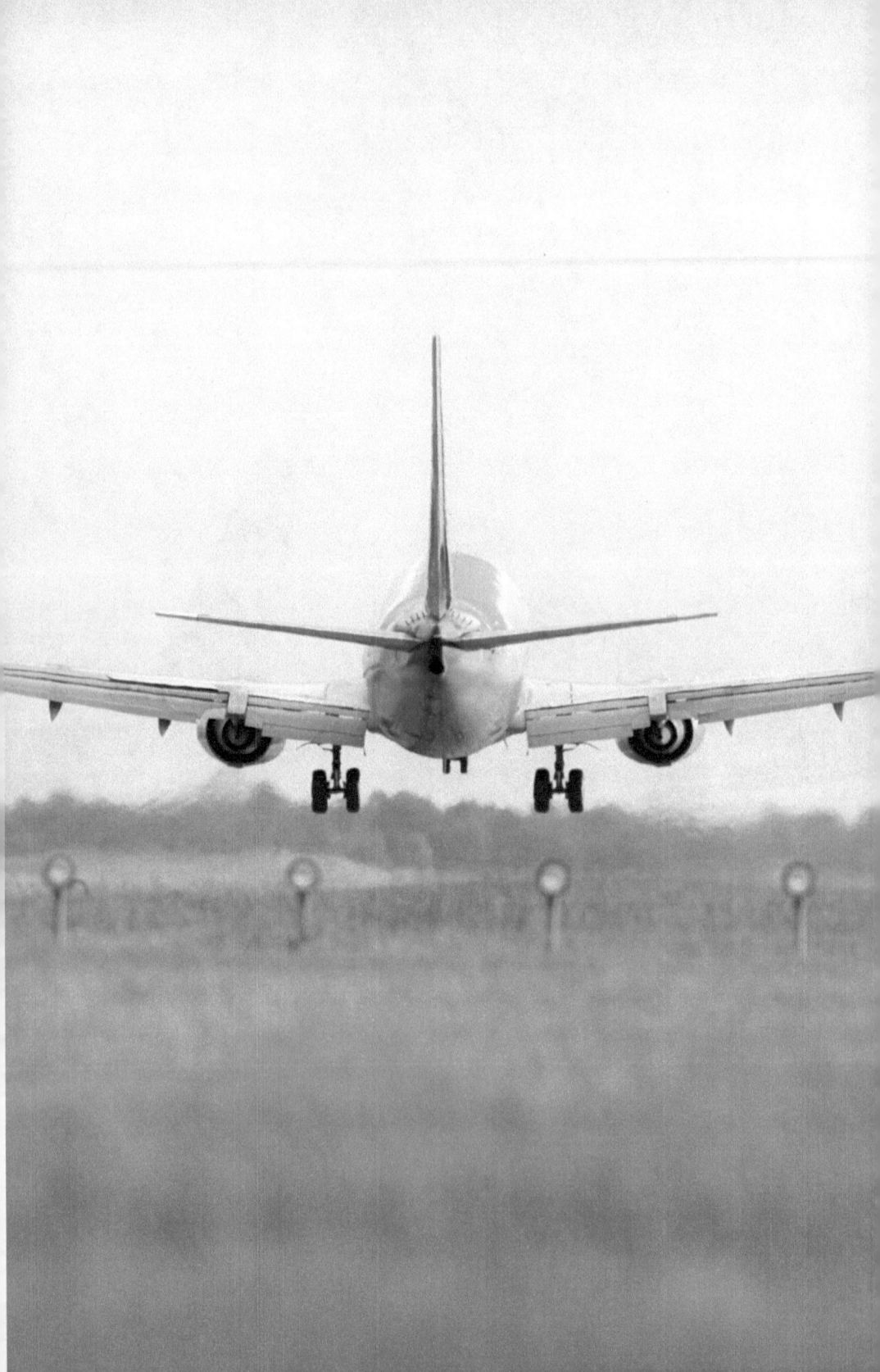

"Use the wings of the flying Universe,Dream with open eyes;See in darkness."

Dejan Stojanovic

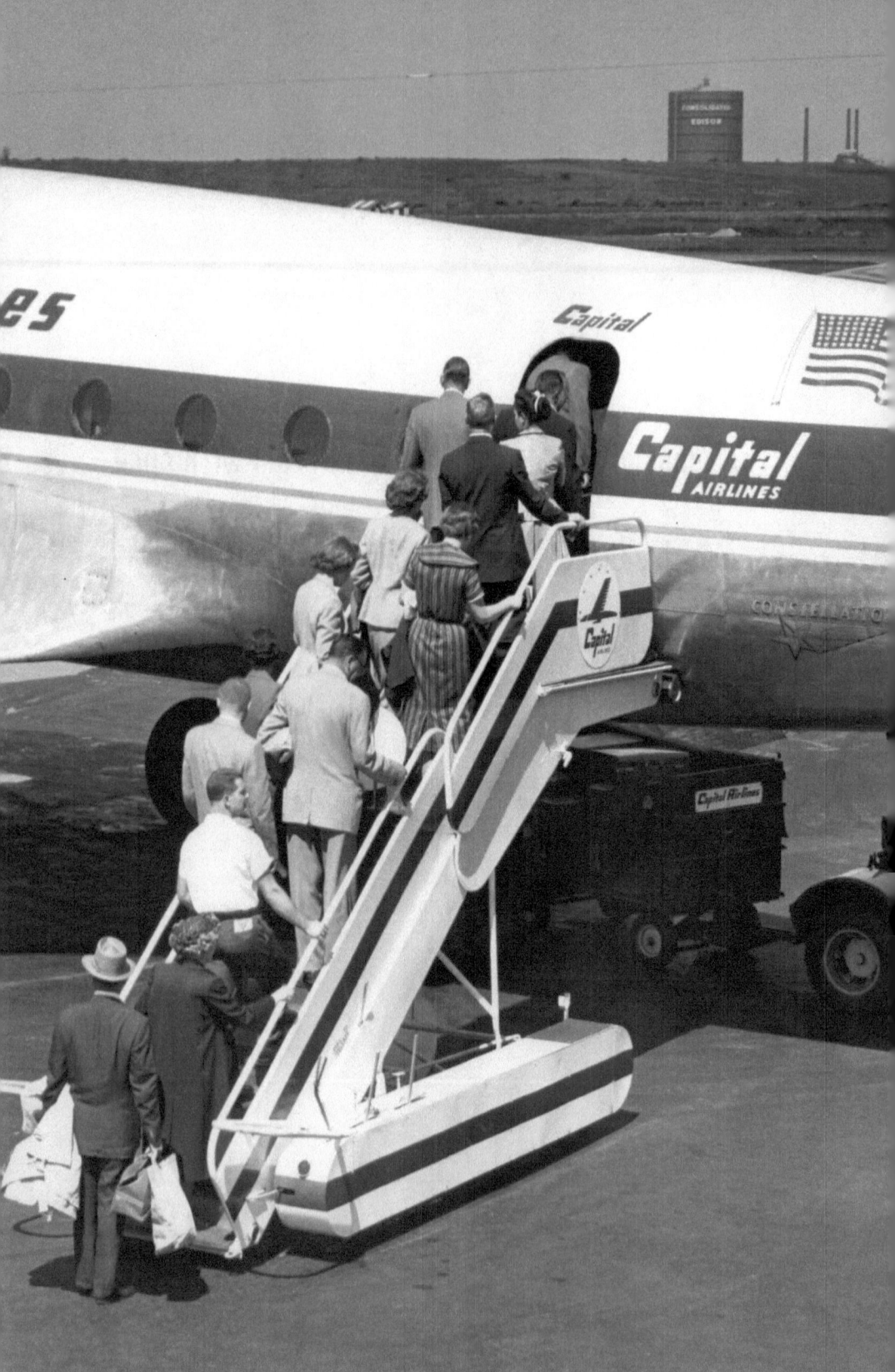

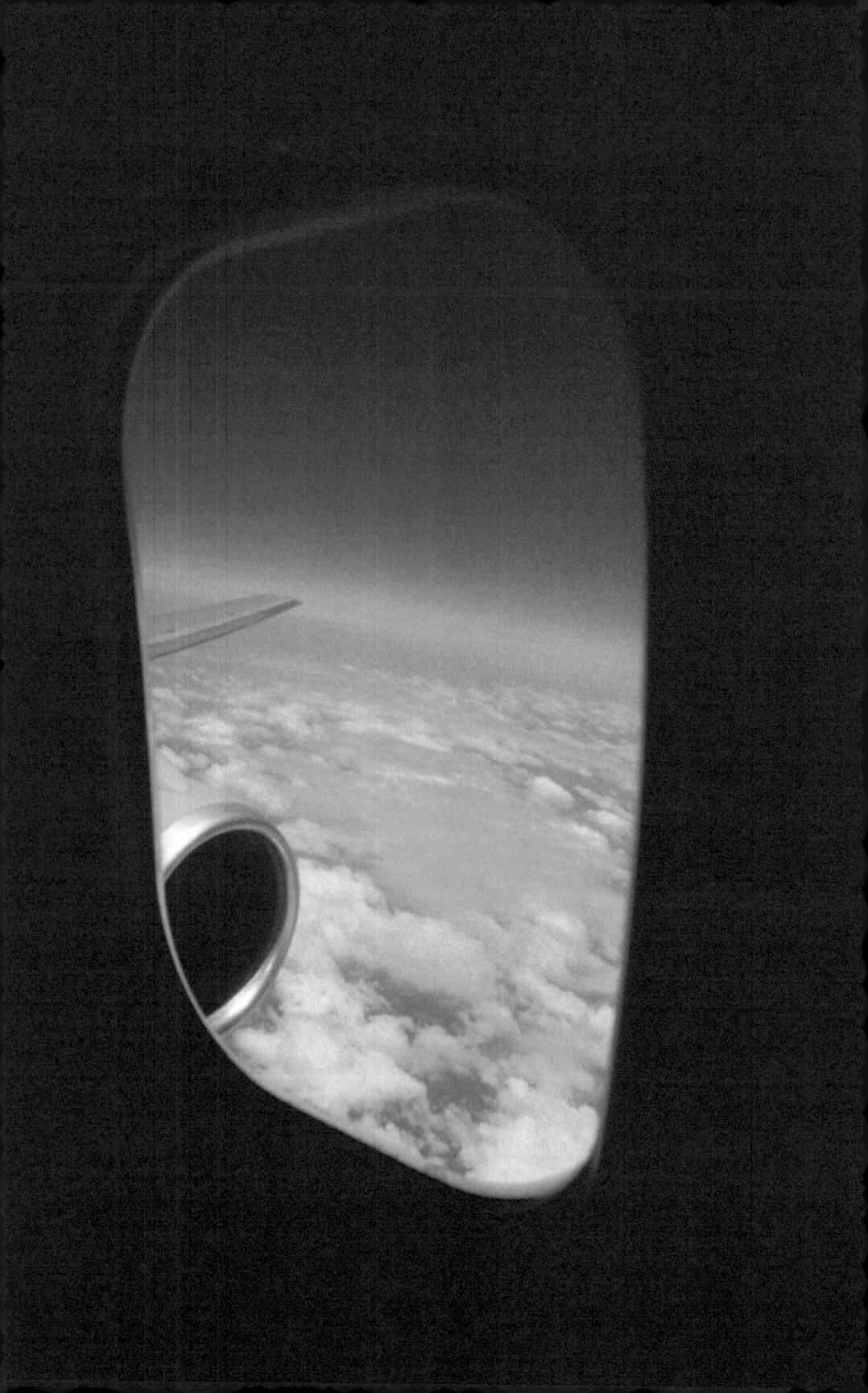

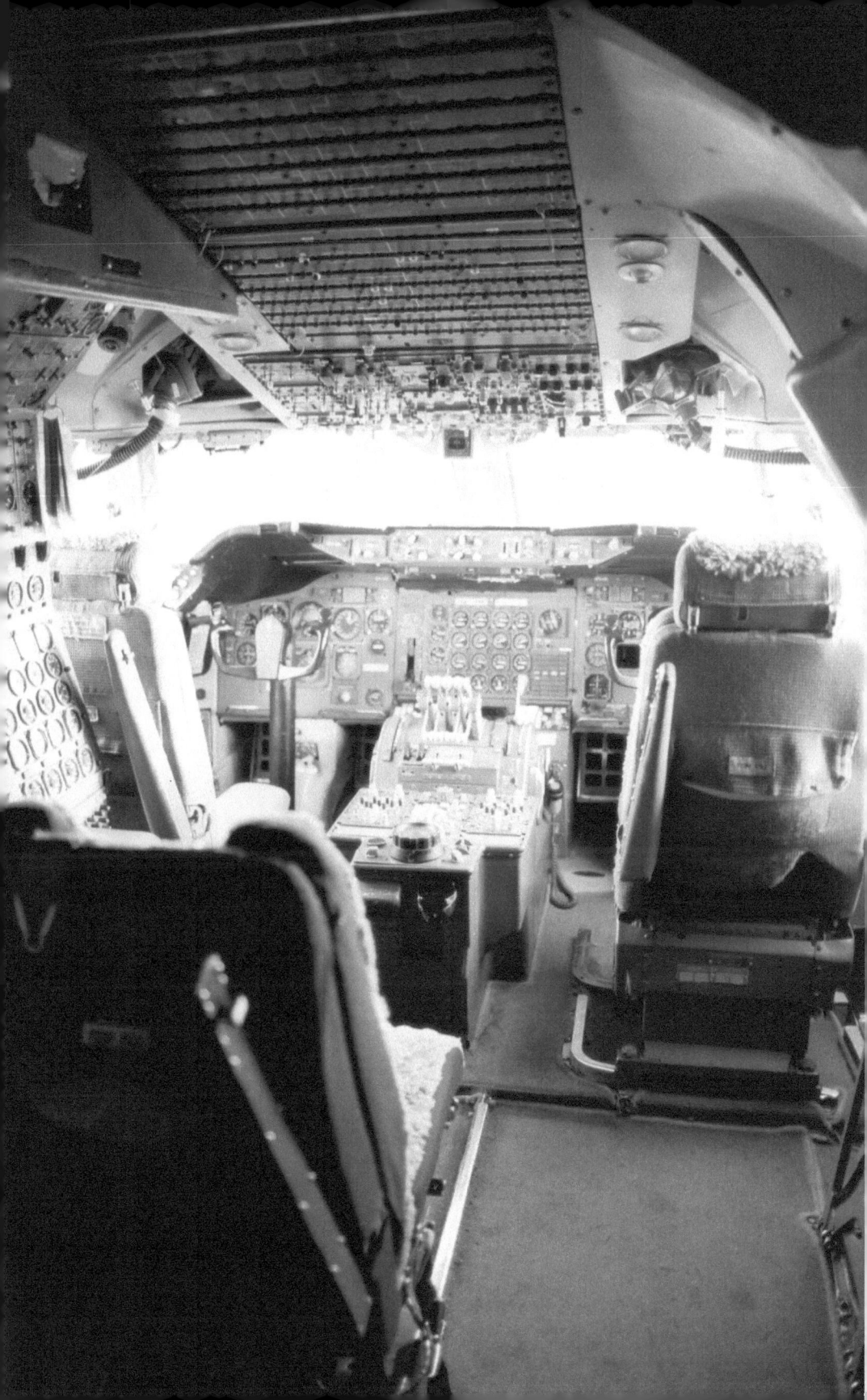

"Thank God men cannot fly, and lay waste the sky as well as the earth."

Henry David Thoreau

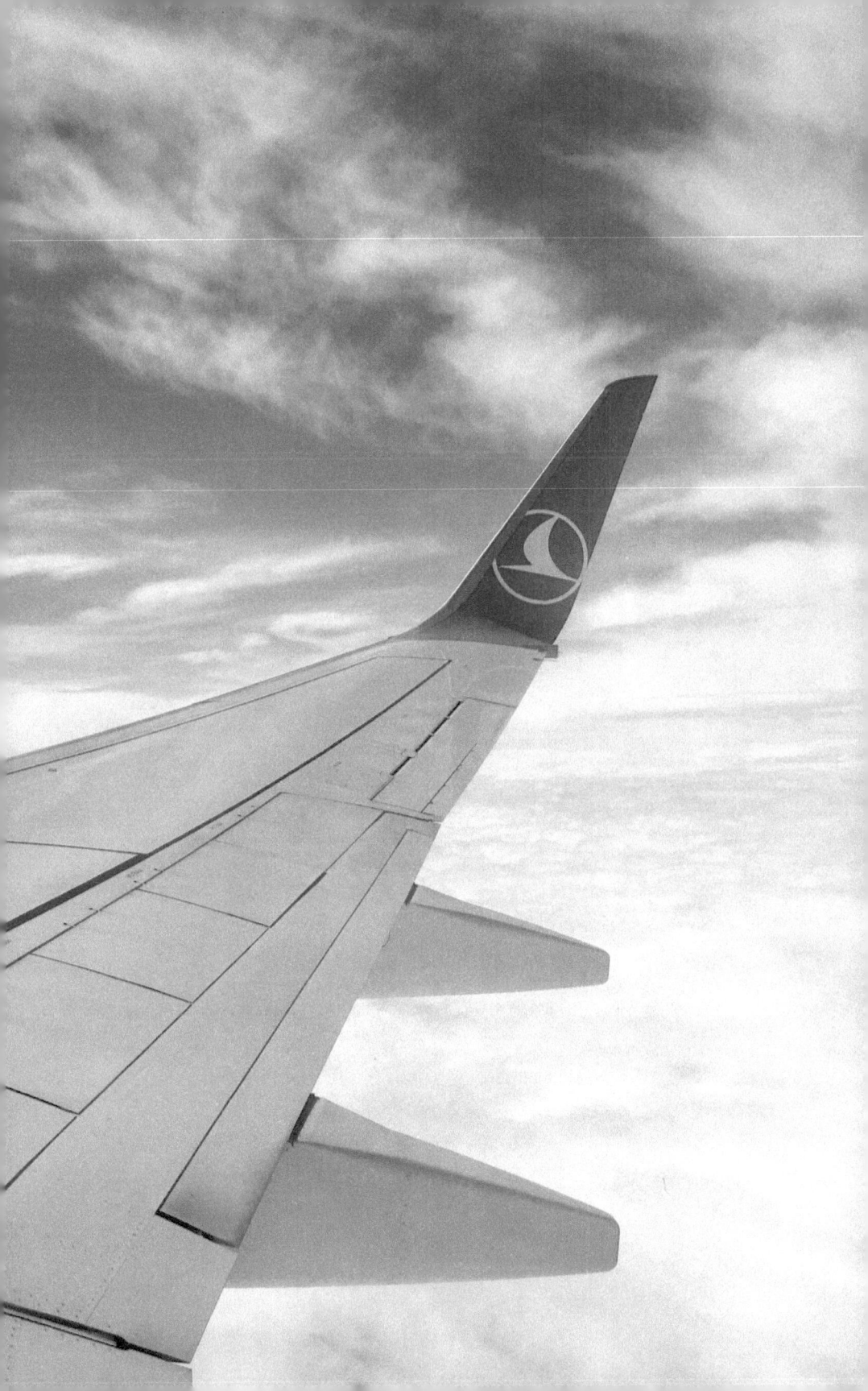

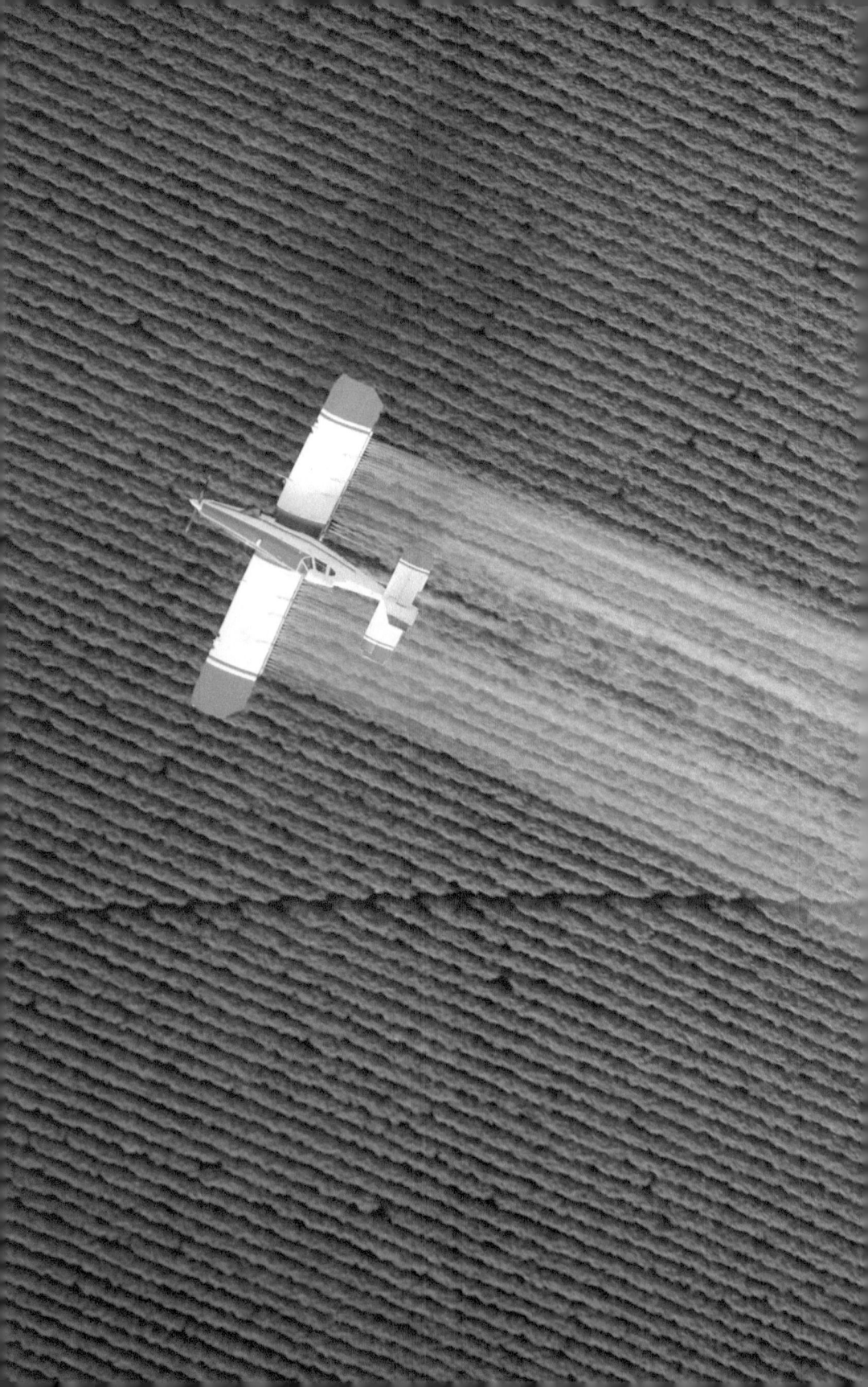

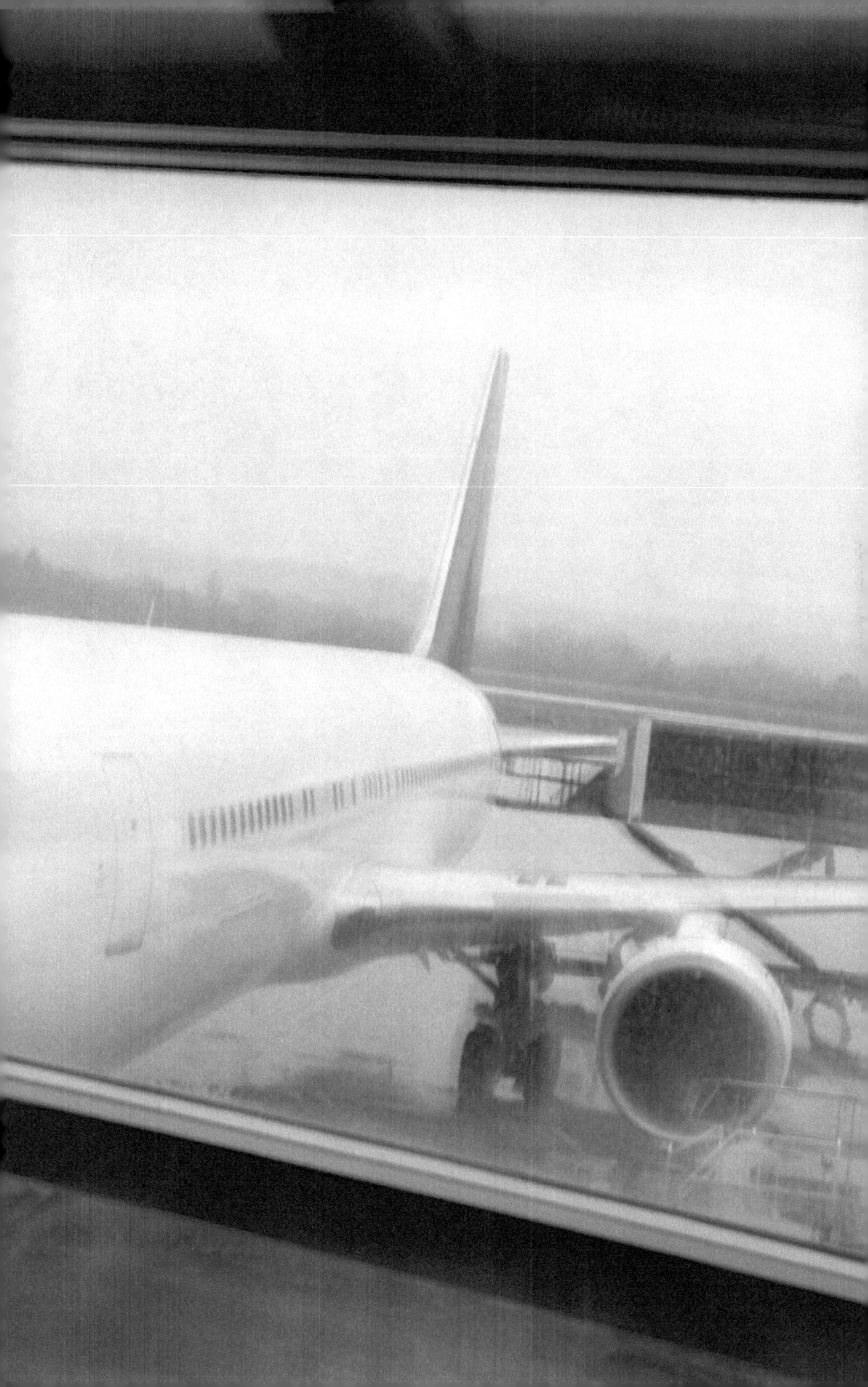

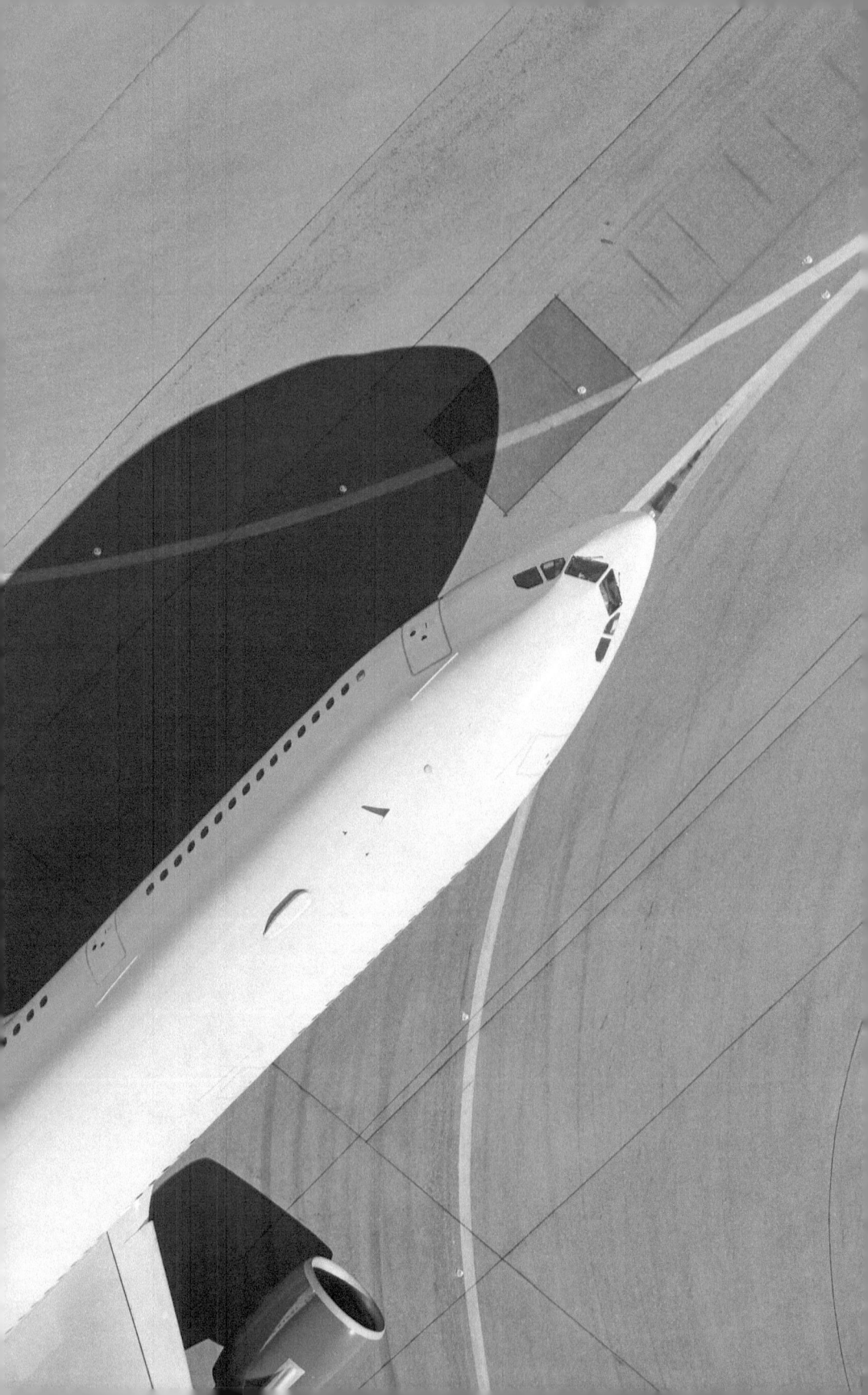

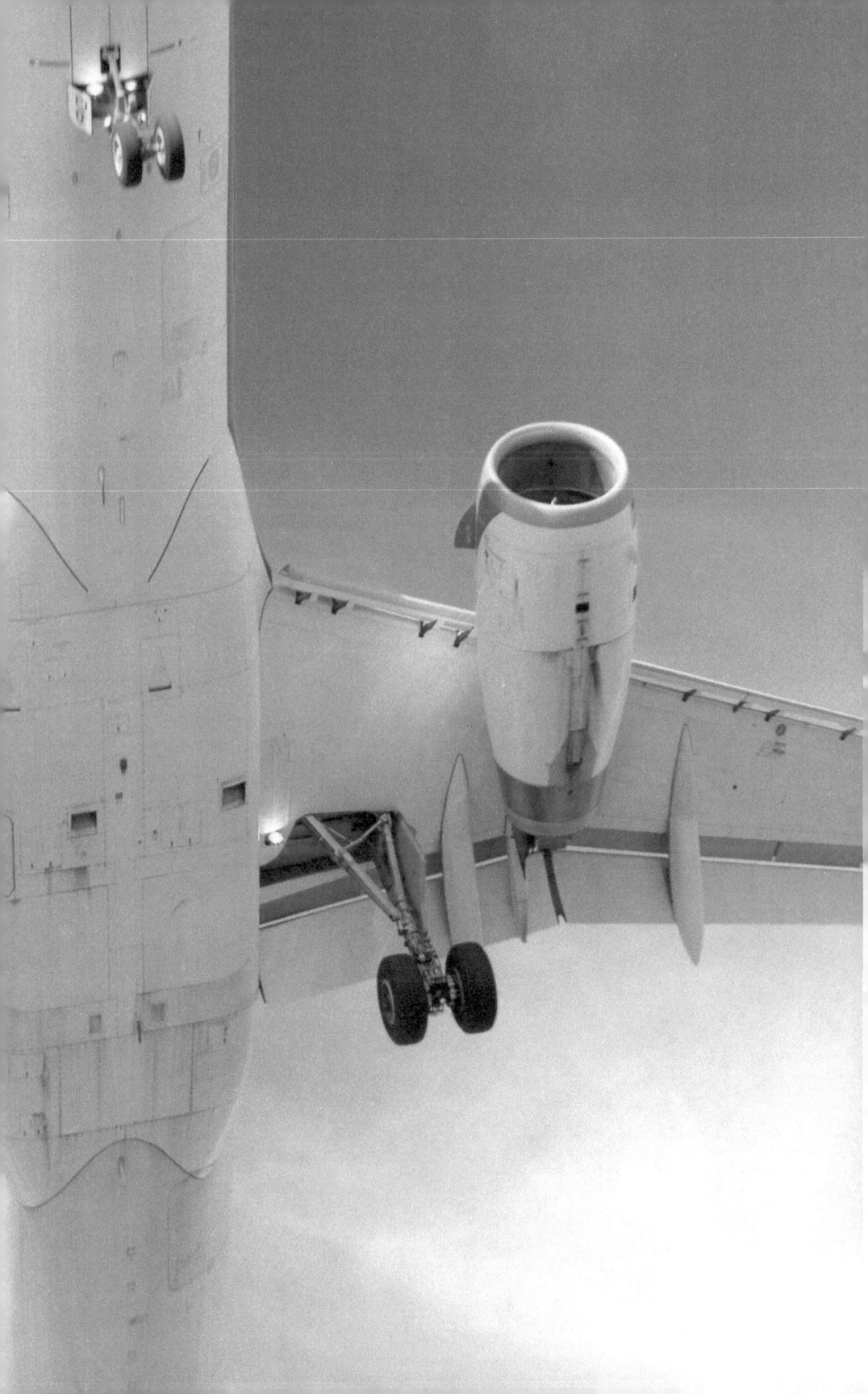

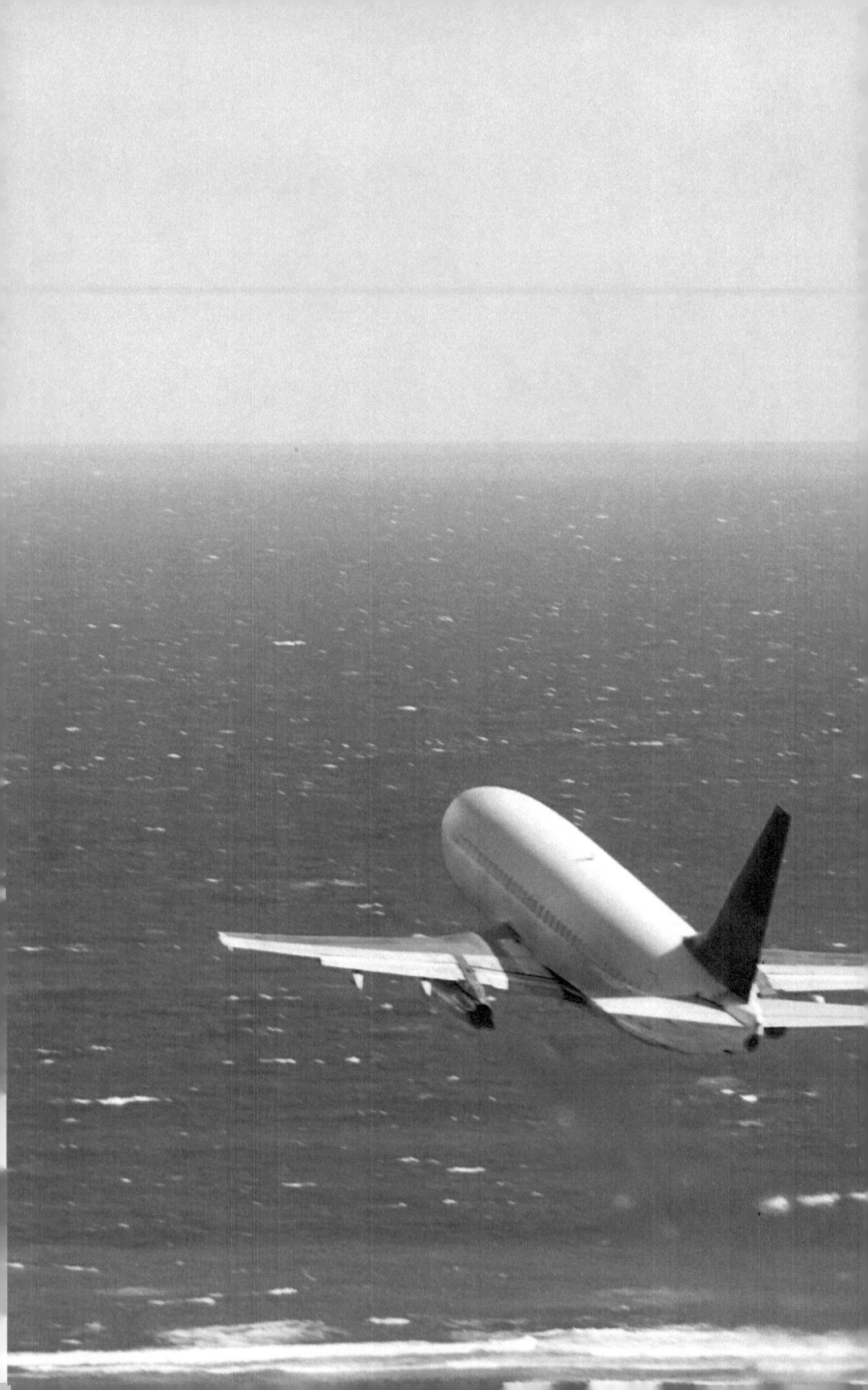

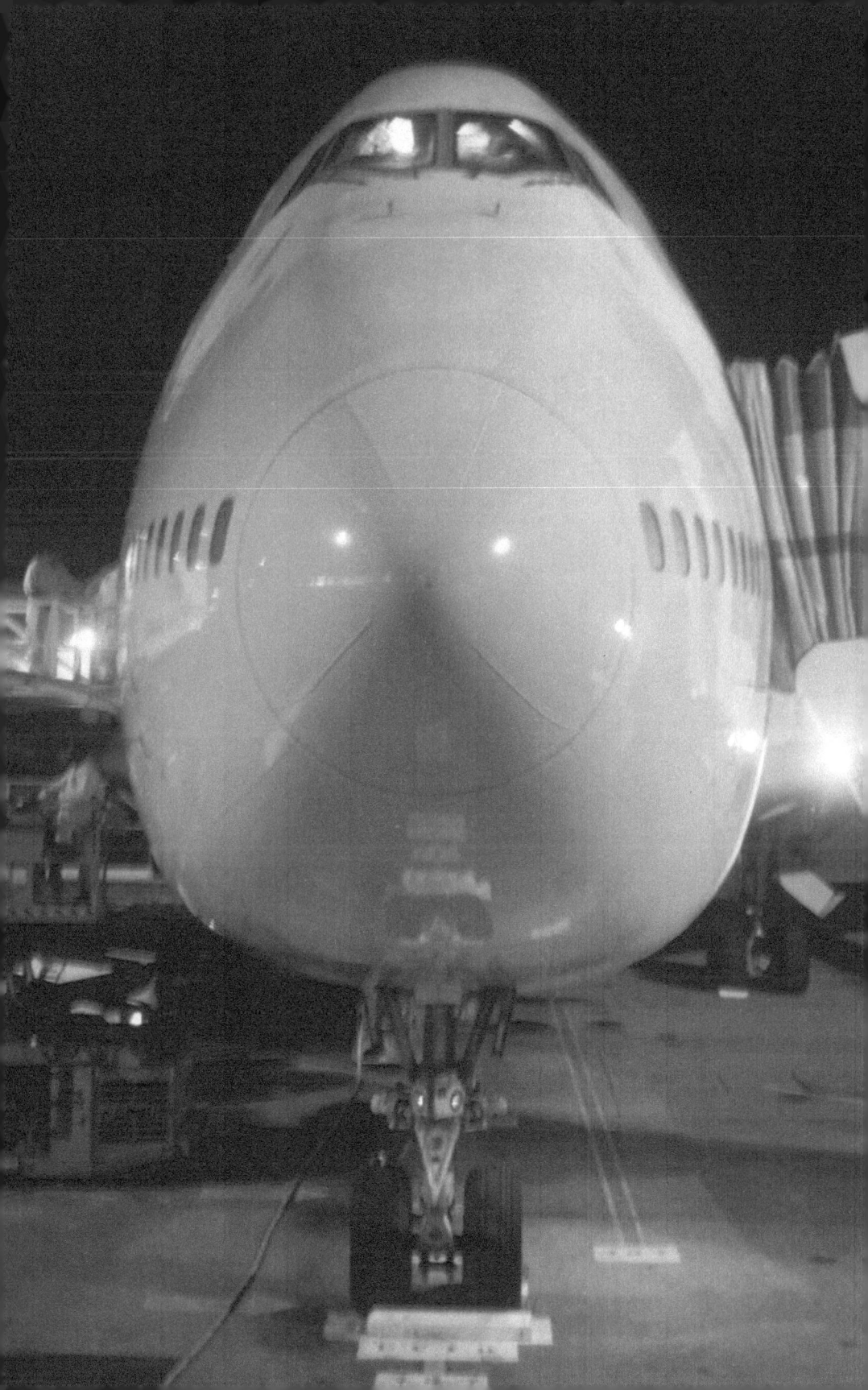

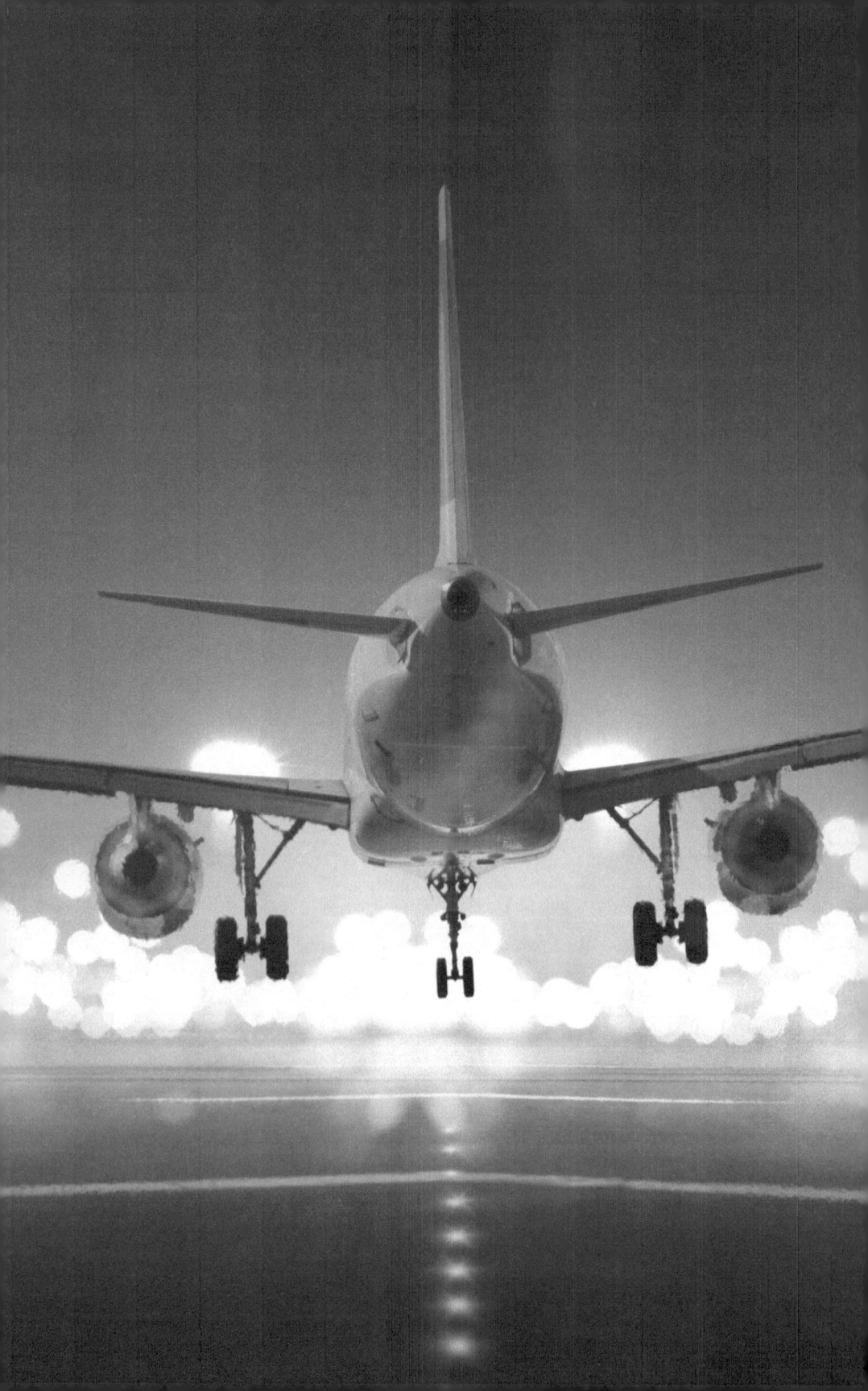

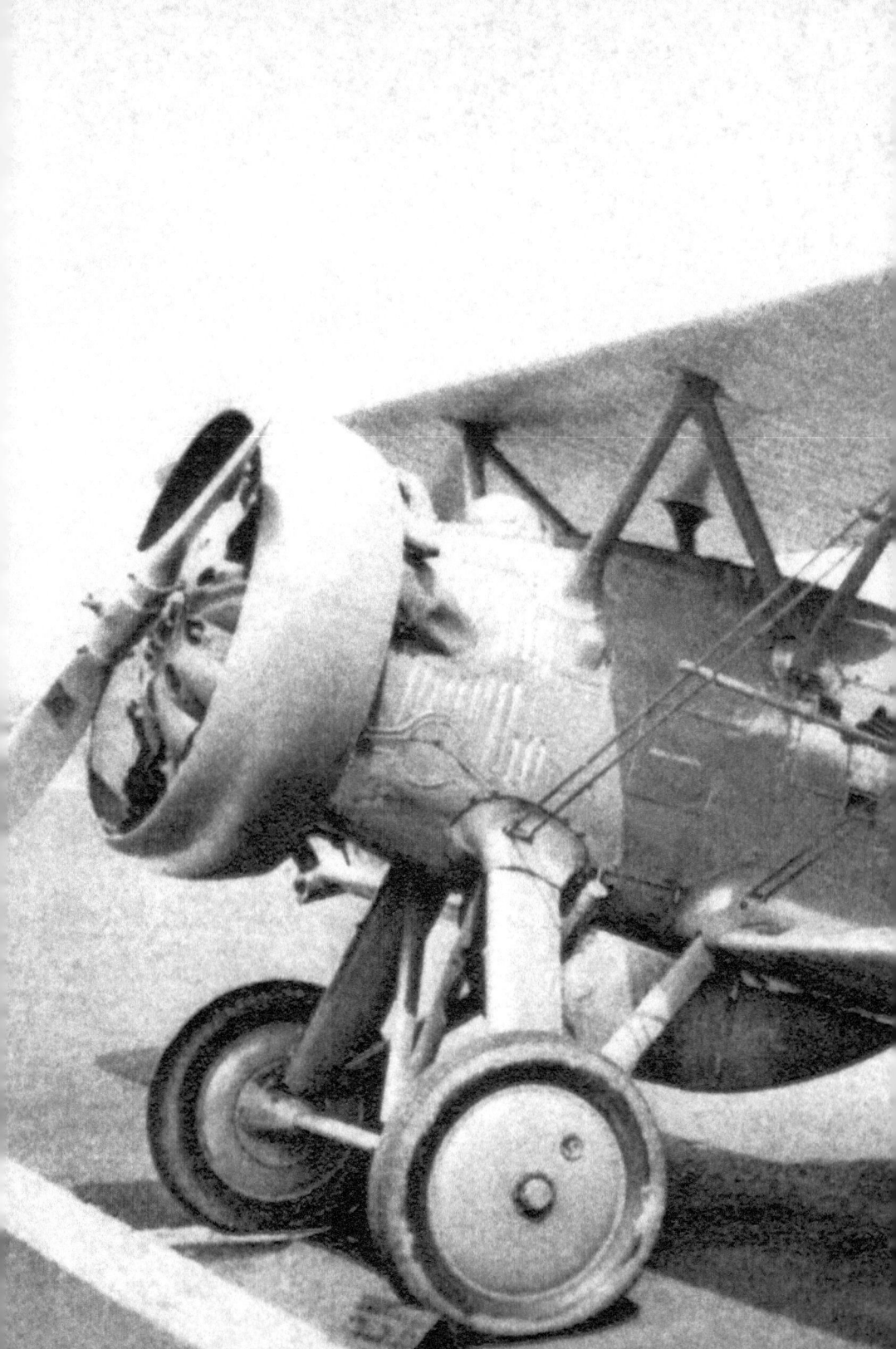

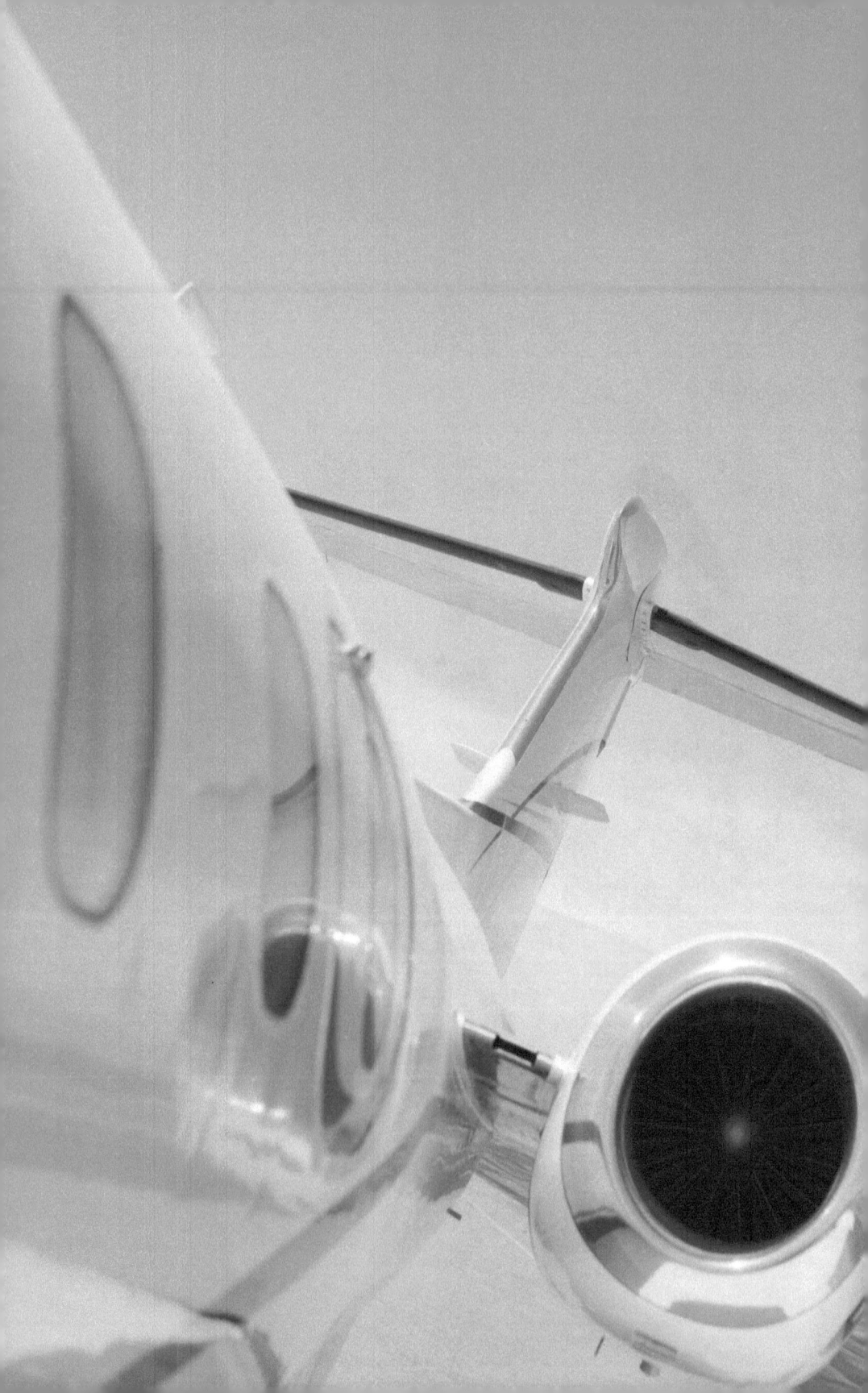

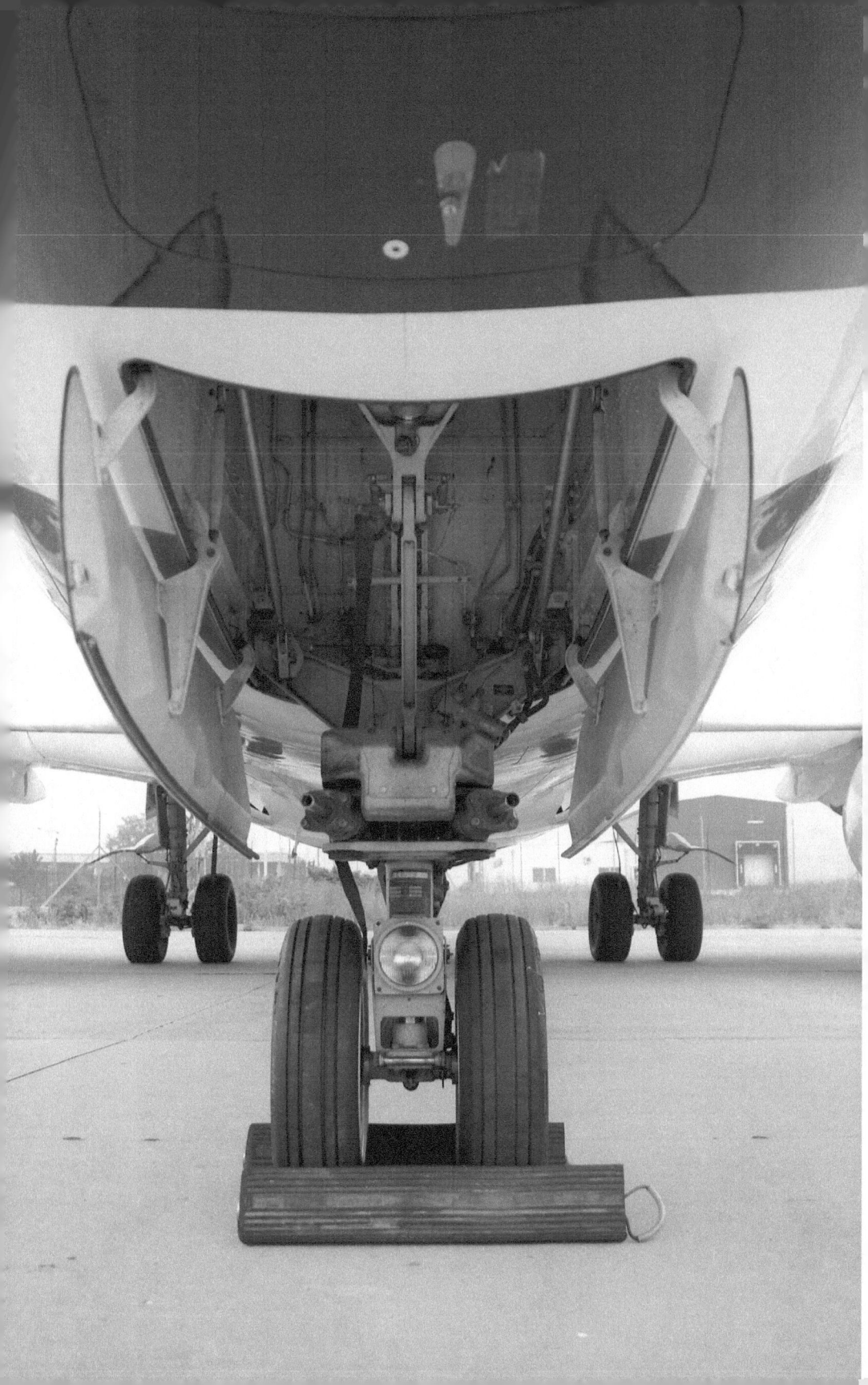